Refiguring in Black

For
Thabang

Refiguring in Black

Tendayi Sithole

polity

First published in 2023 by Polity Press

Polity Press
65 Bridge Street
Cambridge CB2 1UR, UK

Polity Press
111 River Street
Hoboken, NJ 07030, USA

ISBN-13: 978-1-5095-5701-1 (hardback)
ISBN-13: 978-1-5095-5702-8 (paperback)

A catalogue record for this book is available from the British Library.

Library of Congress Control Number: 2022948512

Typeset in 10.5 on 12.5pt Sabon
by Fakenham Prepress Solutions, Fakenham, Norfolk NR21 8NL
Printed and bound in Great Britain by TJ Books Ltd, Padstow, Cornwall

The publisher has used its best endeavors to ensure that the URLs for external websites referred to in this book are correct and active at the time of going to press. However, the publisher has no responsibility for the websites and can make no guarantee that a site will remain live or that the content is or will remain appropriate.

Every effort has been made to trace all copyright holders, but if any have been overlooked the publisher will be pleased to include any necessary credits in any subsequent reprint or edition.

For further information on Polity, visit our website:
politybooks.com

Contents

Acknowledgments

This has been a very interesting journey, which I have walked with amazing souls who pushed me with their comments, suggestions, and criticism. I thank Thabang Monoa, to whom this book is dedicated, for pushing my fragmented ideas into this second installment of *The Black Register*. When I was laboring on this book I was in the great company of those whose names are too many to mention. I want to say to all of you that you made an impact on me in ways that you will not understand.

John Thompson, Lindsey Wimpenny, Susan Beer, and the rest of Polity Press team have made sure that this book is a success. Your support, as always, has been unwavering. I want to extend my thanks to anonymous peer reviewers who gave shape to my ideas. Thanks to Wits University Press for copyright permissions to republish, in an extended form, Chapter 1, "Aunt Hester's Flesh," which appeared earlier as "Meditations on the Dehumanisation of the Slave," in *Decolonising the Human: Reflections from Africa on Difference and Oppression*, edited by Melissa Steyn and William Mpofu (2020). Mzwandile Buthelezi, you are the bomb, and thanks so much for gracing this book cover with your work.

I wish graciously to thank Siphamandla Zondi and the Institute for Pan-African Thought and Conversation at the

University of Johannesburg for appointing me as a senior research fellow and for generously funding this book. My thanks also go to the Johannesburg Institute for Advanced Study under the directorship of Bongani Ngqulunga for hosting me as a 2022 writing fellow.

Lindiwe, *ndino tenda maningi. Mwari aku busise!*

Aperture

There must be many and different ways of redefining the current conjuncture by way of refiguring.

With the emphasis on specificity, refiguring in black can be defined as doing things differently and deliberately so from the black point of view. Precisely at this specificity, there lies the critical mode of thinking about black figures and studying them differently. In this meditation, Frederick Douglass, Toni Morrison, Hortense Spillers, and Charles Mingus are figures who are not only located in black thought but they are thematized outside the conventions of their critical reception and commendation, which means they cannot be studied *otherwise*. By being refigured from the black point of view, this is the insistence that they must be located outside the limitations that are imposed on them as stagnant figures. In short, *Refiguring in Black* has a different tenor and disposition of these figures, hence their refiguring from the black point of view. What is presented here is a meditation by way of refiguring. It is a critical practice, a discourse, whose critical disposition, operation, is (on) the edge. By refiguring, it means that this suite gives new meaning to the thought of Douglass, Morrison, Spillers, and Mingus as in a form of reformulation – rupture. In other words, they are refigured in ways that part company with familiar interpretive practices, discourses, styles, sensibilities, and tropes. Things become radically different.

This, in essence, means seeing things differently, seeing them for what they are, seeing them like never before – say, anew. It is not only seeing just for its own sake. It is the seeing that has been refused, where blackness has been blinded so as not to see things for what they are. It is to see differently and, according to Ngũgĩ wa Thiong'o (1987), it is to see clearly. What does it mean to see clearly? To see clearly is not only to look. It is to have a point of view. It is to see dissimulation and to unmask its falsities, malice, and pretenses. To see clearly is to see differently. It is to see what is not seen. To see clearly is refiguring. It is, according to wa Thiong'o, the institution of a different reality, which comes into being by means of having seen things differently because they are seen from the perspective of the black. For wa Thiong'o, there should be a look at what deformed the black, and that means having to come into confrontation with what deforms and liberates the self from this deformation. It is *to begin anew*. To see clearly, ways of seeing differently, mean coming into contact with what has always been hidden from sight. Not that what is seen is kept off sight. For it is something that is there on sight to see but the black is blinded not to see. Thus, it is as if things are invisible, while they are not. They are there; it is just a way not only of seeing differently, but of seeing clearly after the black has removed the blindfold.

At the moment of this opening, a foundation is laid, and the claim is made that refiguring in black is a distinctive point of view, which, in itself, as radical, presents an opportunity to do things differently, to see them in distinctive ways, to feel them otherwise and, more precisely, to be free to inhabit the realm of the unknown. This is what the work of Douglass, Morrison, Spillers, and Mingus is all about. More so, refiguring their work, and that being done from the black point of view, illuminates the darkened spaces that have decentered these figures and the concerns they bring.

To see in darkness is not to see clearly without any light, or if what is seen is clearly visible. The way of seeing is the call to end blindness. The black must see clearly, and this means seeing what W. E. B. Du Bois (2015 [1903]) calls the "color-line," which is the fundamental problem, and which even went beyond what was marked as the scene of the twentieth century. The clear mark of the world is what Boaventura de Sousa Santos (2007) calls the "abyssal line." Linked to this also is seeing, at the level of alterity politics, which perpetuates coloniality through the paradigm of difference, and which V. Y. Mudimbe (2003) calls the "fault-line." All these aforementioned lines are drawn not on sand, but are engraved on the crust of the earth. At the somatic level, they are drawn all over the racialized body of the black, even more visibly, in the psyche that is fabricated and abstracted by dehumanization. These aforementioned lines, after being seen for what they are, metamorphize, and embody what Nelson Maldonado-Torres (2007) refers to as "lines of damnation." These are the lines that demarcate those who embody life and those who are denied this life.

In this refiguring, Douglass, Morrison, Spillers, and Mingus are engaged in themes that do not account for the totality of their work, but themes that will illuminate different ways of thinking about them. That is why this refiguring is contrapuntal in nature. If there is a grain, this radical instantiation thinks, reads, scripts, and discourses against this grain. The whole idea of this refiguring is, as a practice and disposition, to engage in the open field that black life is – rupture.

Thus far, the incessant and necessary effort of black thought is what has stood in its own name, and no form of interdiction has claimed absolute totality in obliterating it. The way in which refiguring in black is articulating itself has been a forced grammar, a matter of struggle, a matter of necessity. The point is that black thinkers have been doing the thinking, while they are refused the very idea of thinking. They are interdicted when it comes to matters of thought and, as a contrapuntal gesture, they radically refuse and radically insist on doing the thinking from their own black point of view. This, in short, is what refiguring in black means. For, as its imperative, it does the work of grasping and grappling with matters of thought in different registers and dispositions that are fundamentally black. Definitely, this is refiguring in its contextual definitional form, the dispo-sition of this meditation. There is a different accent through which things are thought, and refiguring is such a form. It can also be said, in relation to the forms that dominate the current conjuncture, that refiguring is the disfiguring of forms (more especially if they orthodoxically insist on closure as opposed to rupture).

There is no refiguring in black outside black thought. Already at work is black thought as the constitutive element of black life. The questions, concerns, and matters of black life are confronted by way of refiguring in order to under-stand the critical conjuncture the black is in. Making sense of reality and the world as it were, refiguring in black signals the generativity through which existential concerns have erupted in different and profound ways. This meditation, at this current conjuncture, is one of the ways (among many other dispositions), by way of refiguring, that black thought is taken up. By doing this, through Douglass, Morrison, Spillers, and Mingus as figures of black thought, refiguring in black is heightened into one of the dispositions through which the black point of view is made bold and manifest in the arena in which it has been rendered mute, irrelevant, banal, and all things outside "standards."

To say refiguring in black is to attest to what is not in the name of what is lying out there. Rather, it is a phenomenon that is lived, it is in the current conjuncture of the past and the present. It is the radical work of those who live in their current conjuncture, and who not only make a difference, but who act out of necessity as opposed to acting from luxurious choice. The conditions in which they find themselves have fundamentally to change not by chance, but by pure inten-tions of their making, their radical effort. They are more about pushing limits. In other words, Douglass, Morrison, Spillers, and Mingus do refiguring in black as what is vast and ever-expanding in its grammar, what is impure in its genealogies, trajectories, and horizons, which, in themselves, attest to the complexity of reality as such.

At the heart of this refiguring is Cedric Robinson (2000), whose concept of the black radical tradition is its very edge, and is the operation of how black thought unfolds. It is that critique of Western civilization, the elementary definition whose mode of operation is fundamental as it attests to the material and the concrete, whose abstractions and poetics are not a luxurious muse, but are having to grasp and grapple with different ways of meditating about black life through the criticality of Douglass, Morrison, Spillers, and Mingus. This, to Anthony Bogues (2010), has been the question and concern of what it means to live inside empire. These four figures are those whose thought and life is in the clutches of this empire. It is in this location, however, that insurgent forms of black life are acted and re-enacted to become a radically different reality. Douglass, Morrison, Spillers, and Mingus are within the black radical tradition. In emphasizing the deliverance of the black radical tradition, Fred Moten (2013: 237) points to its "radical resources," which should be mobilized, ones that "lie before the tradition, where 'before' indicated both what precedes and what awaits, animating our times with fierce urgency." This is where generativity lies, and it is what marks the critical thought of Douglass, Morrison, and Spillers. And, as Moten signals, this is a way of tapping into the resources that lie before the tradition. These resources are not what the work of these thinkers is all about, but are matters of black life that can be thought in relation to their own thought.

One important thesis of this meditation is not the interpretation of Douglass, Morrison, Spillers, and Mingus; rather, it is thinking along with each of them by paralleling them with thematic concerns that are appellative to their thought. This is necessary in this refiguration because it opens other domains of thinking that are necessary not only to excavate the relevance of these figures but to attend to what they thought and to show how that is the very extension of black life through what Robinson (2000) calls "ontological totality" in its heterogenous forms. Since black life is not a homogenous totality, what is aimed at here is understanding the ways through which the accounting of this life is what is lived to the limit of having its humanity questioned. It is at this limit that there are those generative forms that insist on living in ways that are not submitting to the imposed status of dehumanization. Douglass, Morrison, Spillers, and Mingus are thinking through the limit, and they are not reduced by it, nor are reduced by it. If thinking freedom is what they can be said to be doing, in the spirit of the black radical tradition, they are engaged in insurgent forms that are concerned with what is urgent.

Urgency and insurgency abound, the edge through which things are being pushed on, at, to, and through; the fact is that there is a lot at stake. This, then, equates to the amount of work to be done, for that work having been done in the past, and which is also to be done in the future – that is, doing the work, refiguring in black, which, in its essence, is not palatable to the captive logics of what is orthodox. Breaking free from the strictures and edicts of what deny humanity, Douglass, Morrison, Spillers, and Mingus think about the modes of being otherwise. To be on the edge, refiguring things, and from the black point of view is, according to Moten (2013: 239), "enforced when we emphysemically authorize ourselves to speak of the spirit of the age." This is the refiguring in black done by Douglass, Morrison, Spillers, and Mingus, who are, as black thinkers, living, thinking, and working in the name of the spirit of the age, thus insisting on breathing from the scarcity of breath. Therefore, the spirit of the age they have been in has been forever critical; refiguring in black is their radical fold and, added to this, their formation. As a result of this, and having to point to the centrality of the edge, it is important to consider the ways in which the spirit of the age are a matter of their urgency and insurgency.

In figuring out the problematic, by way of refiguring, at its edge, it is justified for Douglass, Morrison, Spillers, and Mingus to be central to this disposition, that different outlook, altogether. That is why, for Nahum Chandler (2014), refiguring is the discourse – one that is formulated and enacted as heterogenous. The edge is where things are pushed to/toward. Things will, as a result, be a different form and formation. Walter Mignolo (2011: 321) writes: "Certainly, to move in such a direction is not easy." The move of those whom Mignolo describes as doing "border thinking," and pushing the margins to the edge, is necessary and more urgent. By pushing and blurring the margins, by being on the edge and being disentangled in trappings of colonization, Mignolo makes an indictment of civilization by calling it the "civilization of death."

Douglass, Morrison, Spillers, and Mingus insist on living. They seek to repossess that of which they have been dispossessed. All they seek, from their black point of view, by that edge called the black radical tradition, is to necessitate the possible in the clutches of impossibility. That is why, for Robinson (2000), it is key to define the black radical tradition as the critique of Western civilization. This definition points to the insurgent force that animates the critique of decadence – that is, this Western civilization that has been extracting and disposing of black life. In this definition, the black radical tradition, its insurgent force, that relentless critique, constitutes that generative force that does not come from exhaustion, failure, and defeat. In fact, from what seems to be the end, generativity begins things differently, anew. There is no repetition of the same, but the doing of the *otherwise*. This is the generative force whose grammar of being summons *being to come, being-in-becoming, becoming being*. The self-making of the black is a result of insurrection from the condition of having their humanity denied. It is the self not creating the individual subject, but the totality of black life. It is the life that is at stake, under attack, under siege, captive life whose death is seen as just and justified. The refusal of the black to concede to these criminalizing and pathologizing justifications of death has called for the ways of creating the world in the ways that the black in the existential struggle deems fit. Eruption and disruption are the operative modes through which Douglass, Morrison, Spillers, and Mingus are taken.

This diagnosis, interrogation, and investigation, in the form of an iteration, adjusts to an interest that radically insists on ways of thinking outside the captive logics of this civilization. What Douglass, Morrison, Spillers, and Mingus do is thinking, what they think, and how thinking is done. Their thought demands the effort that is always ready to reformulate. It is clear that in this operation, they engage what Jean-Luc Nancy (1996) refers to as "effectuation," where the creation of the concept emerges from critical thought and where things are given another modulation. This means, as Nancy (1996: 110) states, that "which does not imitate the other, which does not represent it or signify it, but which effectuates it in its own way." The way things are put forth, the way they are argued, that is the place where blackness is – the edge. This is engaging thought, according to Chandler (2014: 85), in "a noncategorical way." This is breaking from and breaking form. To reach and to be at this limit is having to deal with concrete contradictions that haunt dehumanization, and that also cascade into pathologizing the black as the *exteriori* of the human.

Douglass, Morrison, Spillers, and Mingus insist on the otherwise and, by way of a disposition that refigures, their intention is to reschedule critique. The rescheduling of critique comes through what Moten (2018a) pushes forth as "meaning of things," which means the radical disruption of things themselves. It is in this distinctive form that refiguring is put into operation.

To reconfigure is to forge, to make something, otherwise. Also, it is to forge ahead. It is, by way of Nancy's effectuation, which is to say, "explication," the edge. It is to form, set-up, build, establish, invent, and so on. All this makes everything to be on the edge. But, on the other negative hand, to forge is to defraud, falsify, counterfeit, imitate, duplicate, and so on. But here, in this intervention, to forge means to refigure. Whatever the meaning of the forge is, the black engages in the first order of its meaning, the positive one, if you like. That is to say, it is the one that creates possibility.

The black is going where life is. It is this wandering, according to Sarah Cervenak (2015), which forges a set of conditions that necessitate life and the call for it to be lived, freely, even. This is the life that the black must invent. It is not the one that will be given, but what the black will take for having been dispossessed of it. Thus, this is the life that is refigured in black. In short, black life.

What is at stake in so far as the grammar of the black is concerned? The stakes are high. It is the naturalization of racial difference, and this difference means creating the human and the non-human. It is the production of the non-human that creates the conditions of death in a way that is legitimate.

There is that talk of those who are within, the inside thing, *interiori*. It is the talk that happens in private. It is, as Moten (2013) states, a "critique of privacy." It is here that the enclosure should not be the norm. It is a private affair that is challenged; there is something going on that should not be in the private domain. Those who are communicating with each other, in their bond, their filial relation, do so to bring meaning into the world that has denied them any sense of meaning. They are giving themselves something that has been taken away from them. It is their duty to do so, and no one will act on their behalf. Everything is upon their shoulders; it is the burden they carry, their own.

Douglass, Morrison, Spillers, and Mingus engage in the re-cartographization of the world. It is their inscriptions onto maps (re-mapping), that perpetual rewriting on the surface of the map, that makes the map into the visual representation of the place the black inhabits. The world that is under the command of the black inscription is, as a matter of fact, the one that is being made under the tireless effort of having to realize fundamental change. This, for Chandler (2014: 167) is "marking the limit of the world," and it is at this critical edge that refiguring engenders ways in which Douglass, Morrison, and Spillers are thought. The world is made to be in another form. It is the world that is refigured in black, by blacks, not only as interlocutors but as co-creators. The change this inaugurates, as the result of the radical demand for the world to be different, does not have to be a form of coming to the uniform consensus, but of putting to work, the working out of differences, of not only figuring out, but of refiguring. The world must be different, the refusal of the status quo of antiblackness, is what this black radical tradition is all about. This tradition brings the refusal to concede to the order of things, by doing things differently, to seek the disorder of things, to find a new dimension of how things should be, and not reordered – to return to *tabula rasa*. In short, there must be a new beginning. The foundation must be dug again, and maps must be redrawn without borders. The cartographic inscriptions should be the ones of life, and not the imperial domination of Man to the world.

The beginning of being human, the status that has been taken away from the black from birth right until death, is reclaimed and the humanity that is assumed is not the one of the world that has to do with the logic of hierarchization where, according to Anthony Farley (2005), the asymmetrical relations are that of white-over-black. The descriptor, the very analytic, the focal point of critique, is that of diagnosing what dehumanization does, and what are its mechanics. What Douglass, Morrison, Spillers, and Mingus do is the undoing of dehumanization. It is the undoing of what has been the activator of their denial of being. In essence, it is the undoing that will take the initiative of doing, the critique that animates this refiguring as the refusal to be complicit in dehumanization. This is the refusal to go against themselves and their kind.

This way of seeing, and that being a different way, of course, opens this meditation with the conception of the aforementioned aperture. In this formulation, also, there are three meditative installations. The first is "Aunt Hester's Flesh," which is the witness account that Frederick Douglass gives about the horror of slavery. It is the focus of Aunt Hester's horror that her beating can be seen in a way that Douglass gives this witness account of – the captive body that then is abstracted and brutalized as being mere flesh. The second is "The Specter of the Africanistic Presence," which accounts for the ways that Toni Morrison meditates when rewriting the episteme by way of authorizing the figure of the black. This is the radical intervention that refigures how the racialized self, which has been written off or erased from knowledge, gives the authorial inscription that allows the possibility of another to come into being (thus refusing to confine Morrison to being a novelist but, instead, an episte-mologist). The third and last is "Sophisticated Lady – On

Phonographic Authorship," which re-articulates Spillers's writerly practice as attuned to Duke Ellington's composition, and which Charles Mingus re-elaborated. Also, the richness of this intervention makes the critical conjunctures of Spillers and Mingus into an intimate encounter, even if this was not the case – to say what is conjectural in form and spirit.

More specifically, this meditation, as a threefold composition, is a suite. Each chapter is a stand-alone, but in that, it is the re-anchoring of the very idea of refiguring, thus from a black point of view contra dehumanization. These chapters are marked by tempo ("Aunt Hester's Flesh"), acceleration ("The Specter of the Africanistic Presence"), and resolve ("'Sophisticated Lady' – On Phonographic Authorship"). This suite, by means of its threefold composition, distills the spirit that underpins the black radical tradition through the critical operation coined as refiguring in black.

The invitation of this opening, which serves as the narrative arc, calls us to bear witness to what has been, what is, and what will continue to be enclosed and enforced as closure. The compositional experiment, as opposed to structure (the latter which is susceptible to closure), is what is at stake, in so far as what is being witnessed is the very thing with which the world will not concern itself to come into contact with, and *being with* as a mode of not only belonging but dwelling. This is the plight and plague of the black. It is the one that the black should deal with in its own way, a way that is different from the imposed rules and dictations that relegate black thought to nothingness.

1

Aunt Hester's Flesh

There is, at first, that harrowing scene, which is regarded as the primal scene. It is what Frederick Douglass is bearing witness to and what he narrates by giving account of the beating of his aunt. The excess of power, the one that was exercised upon Aunt Hester by Captain Anthony, is the unleashing of death, the very inscriptive force of slavery. This force is a form of inscription, an acute designation, to call it as it is – that is, the marking done on Aunt Hester's flesh through the whip as a writing instrument on her bare back. The horror that Douglass came to witness was his inauguration into the institution of slavery. The inscription of dehumanization is what the whip will signify, the flesh as the site where violence is experimented with and exercised.

The Aunt Hester scene is the one that haunts, and it will continue to be the black condition, the very logic of dehumanization, and about which Douglass does not have language to narrate. It is what defies comprehension, and it is this scene that can be seen as the invention of reality. This is the reality that continues, the one where the black is living in its remnants. This is the scene of unforgetting as it will be a constant reminder throughout the breathing days of black life.

This is not the retelling of Aunt Hester's scene, but an examination of its markings of terror as exercised upon the flesh. The sentient suspension by Captain Anthony is the fatal coupling of scream and blood. The lashes that marked Aunt Hester's flesh, the merciless strokes, which are bloody, gory, and deadly, are the marking of what dehumanization is. The violence that befalls Aunt Hester's flesh is engaged in a form of a radical critique. By giving a witness account of hell, what Douglass rightfully deemed slavery to be, is the true account not only of himself, but of those who are dehumanized.

The concept of dehumanization will be examined. This will account for the ways in which Aunt Hester's beating is not only Douglass's witness account, but also his critique of dehumanization. This critique is, in fact, a form of diagnosis and its analytics of the flesh are not concerned about the horrors of the past, but the everyday life of the violation of the black. Douglass's intervention is radical in that he could not keep silent. Therefore, as compelled by his principled stance, he chose to narrate. And, by doing so, he also chose to enact another form of possibility through the flesh of Aunt Hester.

The Human Scandal

If the human is a given, then the human exists in the world. In a sense, the human is inseparable from humanity. For there to be humanity there must be life. There is no humanity without life. However, then, the mutual standing of the human and humanity has allowed separation, which then suggests that there can be the human without humanity. The conception of the human has to do with certainty and mastery of the ways of life. The subject that is constitutive, the full subject as opposed to the figure of lacks and deficits is the one that is embodied and is in control of the aspects of existence. The subject is, therefore, the transcendental and free agent, *of its own making*. The subject is not the slave.

First, it is important to ask: What is the subject in relation to the human question? Why the human now? What does it mean to think of the human? Is it that the human and the subject are the same? Or, put simply, what is the human in the matrix of power relations? There are unlimited questions worthy of interest for the figure of the human in the metaphorical and real, form and content, misery and happiness, presence and absence, existence and death, and the like. Second, it is important to claim, in relation to the posed questions, that the human has a relational capacity to the world. There are institutions, structures, and reality as such, that are in full support of the human. The formation of the subject and its constitution is not the preoccupation here; but rather, the human question will be pursued through the critique of the subject. It is this ontological axis that will be dealt with here and it draws from the episode that Frederick Douglass (1995 [1845]) recounts of his aunt by the slaveholder Captain Anthony. It is not the cruelty of this episode that is a preoccupation, but the understanding of the mechanics of dehumanization that leads to the invention of the flesh, where the slave is affixed to humiliation, violence, dehumanization, and death. The silent scandal – the non-human in relation to the slave – is what foregrounds Douglass's critique, which is concerned with the "rituals of killing" as per Josh Rios's (2017) conceptualization. The violence exercised by Captain Anthony is the performance of this ritual. In his standing, he does not see himself as human in relation to Aunt Hester, but as what Rios calls the "imposter god." For the fact that the humanity of Aunt Hester has been suspended well before her mere "disobeying" of her master, and the expectation being that there must be obedience through and through, the command that "slaves obey your masters," this order is perverted as the sovereign one. Those who obey are demanded to do so not from their will, but from the enforcement that they are not humans and must obey.

What is understood to be the human has nothing to do with the slave. The human and the non-human and the imposed ontological axes provide a clear determination of who lives and who must die. The slave exists in the realm of non-existence. Therefore, this existence is not the meaningful one but it is the one of humanity that is put into question. What comes out, then, is the question of the non-human.

What does it mean to think from the positionality of the
non-human? The subject has nothing to do with the existence
of the slave. The question that preoccupies the slave must be
about being prefigured as non-human – the question of life
and death. The burden of life asigns a different weight to the
human (subject) and the non-human (the slave).

> The circumstances which I am about to narrate, and which
> gave rise to this fearful tempest of passion, are not singular
> nor isolated in slave life, but are common in every slaveholding
> community in which I have lived. They are incidental to the
> relation of master and slave, and exist in all societies of slave-
> holding countries. (Douglass 1969 [1855]: 85)

The human question gets suspended on the condition where
those who inhabit disposable forms of life are not regarded
as human beings and everything can be done to them without
any form of consequence. In deploying the concept Vita, a
zone of abandonment, João Biehl (2001) brings something
that is analogous to the plantation or the deathscape called
the antiblack world. There are "these human beings" who
are outside being and who, as Biehl (2001: 131) notes, are
"waiting *with* death." Slavery is the creation of Vita, a zone
of abandonment, where anything can be done without any
form of accounting. Those who are in Vita are those who
are waiting with death because death is their condition of
existence. Those who are structured in the crushing machine
of Vita are subjected to the modalities of violence that makes
it as if it is right for them to be there. The non-justification
of Vita is justified. Those who are in Vita are caught in
a condition that denies them any form of possibility – a
nightmare. Biehl (2001: 133) attests: "There is no other place
for them to go." The slave is there in the deathscape. This
is the place where death is permissible. The ethos of death
underwrites Vita. It is here that Biehl states clearly that the
work of death is made easier. In Vita, death is everywhere. It is
the within and the without. In Vita, the human is suspended.
According to Biehl (2001: 134), "there is no legal accountability to the dying in Vita." The dead are dead and what led

to their death is what cannot be brought before the law. It is just normal for them to die and there is nothing extended to them. Those who are in Vita are nameless and they do not fit any category of personhood, and they have no rights that can be extended to them as they do not exist as humans. "In Vita we are not just looking at isolated individuals who, on their own, lost symbolic supports for their existence" (Biehl 2001: 134).

The "social destiny" of those in Vita is the one of no standing; it is the one of those who *have no* standing and, in the loss of humanity, it is as if they have never had humanity before. It is those who are dehumanized, and their death precedes their birth – that is, "a death in social origin. ... [W]ithout any factors, was capable of ravaging the mind and body of a person" (Biehl 2001: 134). Death is slavery's structure of reality, its lubricant, its constitutive element and Biehl even shows how death is also the paradigm and the apparatus of governance. The weight of death imposed on Aunt Hester is as if death were of her own making. Also, Biehl shows, those in Vita are portrayed as if death is their own cause. Those in Vita are marked by death so that they die with each other. Their place in the "inhuman condition" is regarded as the hell they have just brought unto themselves. Never will the weight of death imposed upon them be made to be the dehumanization that is there to make the black to be, according to Frantz Fanon (1967), in the zone of nonbeing. To be in Vita is to be in what Fanon calls the zone of nonbeing, the non-place, the inhabitable zone.

The human who lives what Judith Butler (2004) calls the livable life is the one who has the currency of being mourned. As if recounting on Aunt Hester, Butler has this to say:

> The demand for a truer image, for more images, for images that convey the full horror and reality of suffering has its place and importance. The erasure of that suffering through the prohibition of images and representations more generally circumscribes the sphere of appearance, what we can see and what we can know. But it would be a mistake to think that we only need to find the right and true images, and that a certain reality will be conveyed. The reality is not conveyed by what is represented within the

image, but through the challenge to representation that reality delivers. (Butler 2004: 146)

Butler is also concerned with how the human, and those who are made less than human become represented. The suffering of the latter is minimized if not erased. These are mysterious ways of being, but which have found themselves to be normalized and thus do not raise any moral ire because they are no longer frowned upon. To be in Vita is to be where ethics and all forms of accounting cannot be extended but only suspended. Biehl (2001: 142) writes: "Vita is a place in the world for populations of 'ex-humans.'" Nobody mourns them. It is the place of remnants, the things of no use or things of no value. Whatever happens to them is what can go unnoticed, unreported, and unseen. The happening that occurs in Vita is a non-happening. For the logic of this is that nothing can happen to that which is nothing. Those in Vita are, according to Biehl, animalized. They are outside the domain of being. In amplification, Madina Tlostanova (2017) states clearly how dehumanization is constructed and structured. Tlostanova (2017: 25) writes: "Large groups of people within this opposition did not count as humans and were coded as belonging to the animal world, and positioned lower in the legitimized chain of being." Aunt Hester, condemned in dehumanization, is made to be, according to Tlostanova, the other who does not exist and without any ontological currency that demands mourning or any form of human compassion.

The question of stakes is always what is high. Aunt Hester is made to fall into the domain of those who can be addressed as if they do not exist.

The structure of address is important for understanding how moral authority is introduced and sustained if we accept not just that we address others when we speak, but that in some way we come to exist, as it were, in the moment of being addressed, and something about our existence proves precarious when that address fails. More emphatically, however, what binds us morally has to do with how we are addressed by others in ways that we cannot avert or avoid; this impingement by the other's address constitutes us first and foremost against our will or, perhaps put more appropriately, prior to the formation of our will. So if we think that moral authority is about finding one's will, it may be that we miss the situation of being addressed, the demands are relayed. That is, we miss the situation of being addressed, the demand that comes from elsewhere, by which our obligations are articulated and pressed upon. (Butler 2004: 130)

Things are much scrappier in Aunt Hester. The will of the slave is one that is not a given but the very deadly thing that the slave must turn into in order to be free. Of course, this is unavailable to Aunt Hester at the moment of her beating. But this will has been there before, as she went against the command of her master. Her merciless whipping is Captain Anthony's declaration of war against that will. He is fighting against the will as it is a mode of self-possession, and that is the very thing that will make Aunt Hester human. Now, in terms of the modes of address, what does this have to do with will? Well, everything. But then, this is only possible in the condition where there is humanity, and where there are asymmetrical power relations and dehumanization. In the addressing of Aunt Hester, who is made a thing at the possession of Captain Anthony, things are certainly scrappier. For her humanity is denied, and how then will she be addressed as being human? Of course, the confirmation is negative in this regard. The human question is not in the equation and the mode of address here is the one of failure – precarity. Butler's insistence on the authoritative mode of address will only be applicable if the humanity of Aunt Hester was not only denied by Captain Anthony, but the whole apparatus of slavery *in toto*.

When we consider the ordinary ways that we think about humanization and dehumanization, we find the assumption that those who gain representation, especially self-representation, have a better chance of being humanized, and those who have no chance to represent themselves run a greater risk of being treated as less than human, regarded as less than human, or indeed, not regarded at all. (Butler 2004: 130)

Aunt Hester falls into the category of the latter. It is not the result of her beating that turned her to be such. From the womb of her mother, who was a slave, she was not regarded as human at all. Saidiya Hartman (2016) presses on the precarity of the womb, and where the prerogative of birth is dispossessed.

> For the enslaved, reproduction does not ensure any future other than that of dispossession nor guarantee anything other than the replication of racialized and disposable persons or "human increase" (expanded property-holding for the master). The future of the enslaved was a form of speculative value for slaveholders. Even the unborn were conscripted and condemned to slavery. (Hartman 2016: 168)

The womb was captured by slavocracy, with the master as the operator. The slave is the slave. There is no child, the mark has been placed on the flesh – the slave is a thing to be possessed and it is dispossessed because it is denied possession even of life itself. There is nothing of the slave because the slave is decreed nothing. Hartman (2016: 169) asserts: "Slavery conscripted the womb, deciding the fate of the unborn and reproducing slave property by making the mark of the mother a death sentence for the child."

> Those black and blackened bodies become bearers (through violence, regulation, transmission, etc.) of the knowledge of certain subjection as well as the placeholders of freedom for those who would claim freedom as their rightful yield. Put another way, the everyday violence that the black(ened) bodies are made to bear are markers of an exorbitant freedom to be free of the marks of a subjection in which we are all forced to participate. (Sharpe 2010: 4)

This even goes to Douglass, who saw the "blood-stained gate," and here it will be submitted that it was not him being touched by slavery, but while he was in the womb of Aunt Hester's sister. The nothing human of Aunt Hester should be understood with modes of being addressed as failure, failure that results from being dehumanized. Those who are dehumanized are not, in slavery, addressed as humans. So, address is denied. To be in the machine, whose inscription is what Christina Sharpe (2016) calls "anagrammatical," means that whatever Aunt Hester *is* means "not being." The arbitrary changing of words, and them having a different meaning, has meant the fabrication of the black being. The word "break" can be altered to "brake," and such an anagrammatical inscription of blackness has a bearing on how humanity is denied. The will of the black in the face of the break and brake, the two as the force exercised outside of blackness, still denote the power that is exercised upon the black. The merciless whipping of Captain Anthony enacts the break and brake of Aunt Hester. This anagrammatical inscription is enduring and it is without duration. Even if she is able to consent to the demands of slavery she is still being violated. She is in the "brutal architectures" of what Sharpe (2016: 115) articulates as "the deathly demands of the antiblack worlds," the apparatus of violence that is designed to render her non-being from womb to tomb. "It is a reminder that to be Black is to be continually produced by the wait toward death; that the cradle and the grave double as far as Black flesh is concerned" (Sharpe 2016: 88). Douglass was enslaved before birth. The black stain gate *qua* Vita is the anteoriginary. This is Vita as designed by Captain Anthony in strengthening the apparatus of slavery. This mode of anagrammatical inscription, this reminder, is the one where its mechanistic form is the reproduction of repetition. This banality of dehumanization, in its consistent, constant, and continual repetition is made to be such in order to create nothingness out of Aunt Hester and to make Douglass see Captain Anthony's power as divine and what will not be defeated. It is this repetition that not only creates monotony, but intensification of sovereign power exercised on the body, mind, and soul of the slave. The fact of offering more trauma, as Sharpe states, is to deny humanity and a way of removing the black outside the category of personhood.

From womb to tomb, Douglass is a captive thing. The whipping of Aunt Hester was his whipping even before he was born. The enslaved body of Aunt Hester's sister – his mother – is the one that is marked with lashes. These lashes not only mark the flesh by drawing blood on it, they rip it apart through merciless lacerations, which to Hortense Spillers (1987) is mutilation and expulsion of the body not only from its corporeal form, but its exclusion from being – that is, the flesh being the antecedent of the body – nothingness. This nothingness even defies any field of abstraction to account for Aunt Hester. Her flesh gave birth to the blood-stained gate *qua* Vita. Sharpe (2010: 7) writes the following about Douglass: "First he was born. Then he was born into the significance of being born a slave, born into a symbolic universe of slavery. Made and unmade in the same moment." This means, for Douglass, and his aunt before him, that there is no exemption.

The reference to nothing, the mode of address that even renders what happened there as nothing – that is, nothing happened because there is no such thing that exists called Aunt Hester. The name can even be collapsed into the name with no meaning. Even her being the aunt of Douglass will be subjected to erasure because Douglass is also in Vita. Those who are in Vita are, according to the eliminationist logic directed against their humanity, those who are not there. They cannot be counted and accounted for. Aunt Hester, in the hands of Captain Anthony's whipping and rapability, is nothing. She is, as a nonbeing, a property of Captain Anthony, who sees it right to lord over her and to do anything he deems fit on her flesh. In fact, she is the edible thing. The predatory and carnivorous force of Captain Anthony means that Aunt Hester is already a meal served – *bon appetit*!

This is the devoured flesh, and it is being eaten by the whip whose insatiable appetite wants more and more. The only thing that can stop Captain Anthony's whipping is not his satisfaction. Douglass (1969 [1855]: 88) recounts: "After laying on some thirty or forty stripes, old master untied his suffering victim, and let her get down." It is his exhaustion, his limit of the anagrammatic inscription, which, should he desire, can restart the whipping again. It is not the injury of the slave that will determine the extent of suffering, but the exhaustion of the hand that holds the whip. There is nothing that is out there for the slave; everything that is out there is against the slave.

Dehumanization is the inscriptive force while the whip as an instrument separates the non-human and property. The whipping of livestock is collapsed with that of the slave. The departure point of this warped logic is the sentient suspension of the slave, who is put together, indexed, calculated, weighed, aggregated, added, subtracted, and counted with all that is the master's property. The killing of the slave will mean nothing in the world that denies the humanity of the slave. The ontological suspension, on top of sentient suspension, means that there is nothing such as the slave in the world of the living. The slave is fabricated to be a thing that can be killed, and nothing can be done about it. The slave cannot be wronged because it is only the human who can be wronged, as there are ontological guarantees that are extended to the human, and the slaves' being in the world is that of relationality.

Frank Wilderson (2003) states clearly that the slave is written outside any form of relationality, and the positionality of the black in the antiblack world is a testament to this. The slave is the category that is written outside the cartographic record, the figure that is, in Wilderson's words "off the map;" the Fanonian on-being, the ontologically depleted. By the force of capture, the emptied will is the one that the slave has to regain again and again in order to stand up and fight. It is not that urgency is already there. It is made to suffer by the anagrammatical inscriptions and the violence that comes with the will of the master, which imposes itself as divine. It is in these sets of conditions that the slave is made to bow and obey the terror of the master, which is not dependent on the slave's wrongdoing. The slave is already wrong. The slave does not have to commit any wrong-doing. The slave is the wrong itself. The master's will is exercised by punishing the wrong. So, in this position, this warped logic of cause, the justification of dehumanization is solidified. The master's will is that unchecked power, that license, that excess, that despotism. The anagrammatical inscription of the break and brake is the master's code and it then gets imposed on the slave. It cannot, in its form and content, apply to the master. Only a thing can be subjected to this anagrammatical inscription. The whip is the instrument of such an inscription. Behind the whip there lies the body that is power itself – the master *qua* master – the sovereign being that the slave must obey and kneel before. For the master is invented to be the decider of the slave's life and death. Put simply, the supreme being, the one and only – master!

The human question does not matter to Captain Anthony. He is the master and, in relation to the slave he sees nothing to be thought of in terms of the human. In giving account of his character, Douglass (1969 [1855]) states how his character change in weather-form vacillates into mildness and gentleness, and also that these traits were occasionally displayed.

> He could, when it suited him, appear to be literally insensible to the claims of humanity, when appealed to by the helpless against an aggressor, and he could himself commit outrages, deep, dark, and nameless. Yet he was not by nature worse than other men. He had been brought up in a free state, surrounded by the just restraints of free society – restraints which are necessary to the freedom of all its members, alike and equal – Capt. Anthony might have been as humane a man, and every way respectable, as many who now oppose the slave system; certainly as humane and respectable as are members of society generally. The slave-holder, as well as the slave, is the victim of the slave system. A man's character greatly takes its hue and shape from the form and color of things about him. (Douglass 1969 [1855]: 80)

This is a very interesting account of Captain Anthony's character. Does it mean, as Douglass claims, that he is different from other slaveholders and he is a victim of the system of slavery? Well, this smacks of nothing but apologia.

> Under the whole heavens there is no relation more unfavorable to the development of honourable character, than that sustained by the slaveholder to the slave. Reason is imprisoned here, and passions run wild. Like the fires of the prairie, once lighted, they

are at the mercy of every wind, and must burn, till they have consumed all that is combustible within their remorseless grasp. Capt. Anthony could be kind, and, at times, he even showed an affectionate disposition. Could the reader have seen him gently leading me by the hand – as he sometimes did – patting me on the head, speaking to me in soft, caressing tones and calling me his "little Indian boy," he would have deemed him kind, old, and, really, almost fatherly. But the pleasant moods of a slaveholder are remarkably brittle, they are easily snapped; they neither come often, nor remain long. His temper is subjected to perpetual trials; but, since these trials are never borne patiently, they add nothing to his natural stock of patience. (Douglass 1969 [1855]: 80)

Douglass is, for sure, at pains to search for the humane traits of Captain Anthony. He miserably fails. This failure, obviously, is owed to the fact that Captain Anthony is the slaveholder. He does not deviate from the protocols of slaveholding. No matter how much Douglass portrays some of the humane gestures, he himself admits that they fall by the wayside. But Douglass stubbornly persists in this failure:

Most of his leisure was spent in walking, cursing, and gesticulating, like one possessed by a demon. Most evidently, he was a wretched man, at war with his own soul, and with all the world around him. To be overheard by the children, disturbed him very little. He made no more of *our* presence, than that of the ducks and geese which he met on the green. He little thought that the little black urchins around him, could see, through those vocal crevices, the very secrets of his heart. Slaveholders ever underrate the intelligence with which they have to grapple. I really understood the old man's mutterings, attitudes, and gestures, about as well as he did himself. But slaveholders never encourage that kind of communication, with the slave, by which they could learn to measure the depths of his knowledge. (Douglass 1969 [1855]: 81)

This stubborn persistence is turned sentimental. It is the one that, wittingly and unwittingly, humanizes Captain Anthony and makes him as if he is a different kind of a slaveholder. Whatever Captain Anthony does, he does it with free will and knowing that, even if the slaves were cunning, they would not do anything in the regime that would solidify his being and strip off everything from the humanity of the slave. The sensibility of his character, which Douglass is at pains to paint, is smudged by the fact that Captain Anthony is a slaveholder. Even if he is born into the so-called "free society" and is on the bloodline of the abolitionists, still, even in that sphere there is dehumanization. The liberal sensibilities that were propagated in the "free society" had nothing to do with the freedom of the slave. Captain Anthony is a slaveholder, the dehumanizer, the one who feasts on the bodily being of the slave. Douglass's apologia, an epistemic and ontological error of note, is separating slaveholders from the system of slavery. Here is Douglass (1969 [1855]: 83): "I think I now understand it. This treatment is a part of the system, rather than a part of the man." The slaveholder is the extension of the system of dehumanization and is so with the full knowledge that there must be dehumanization for the system to be maintained and sustained.

Wilderson (2010: xxi) asks: "What does it mean to suffer?" This question is posed to tear the commonsensical one of freedom apart. Wilderson asks the question at its originary moment, the one which, in itself, will lead to ways of understanding the black condition at the level of diagnosis, in order to avoid the pitfalls of the symptomatic. Wilderson is concerned with the question of black suffering because dehumanization is still intact, and the logic of the world is still fundamentally antiblack. Since there is dehumanization, the sentient suspension being the reigning logic, what about sanctuary? Wilderson is on the negative with this: what lies before the slave is a void. There is nothing to which the slave can reach out. For, as Wilderson states, there are no institutions present to protect blackness, as the whole apparatus of antiblackness feeds itself through black suffering. This is the suffering that Wilderson states defies any measurement and scale. Also, there is no language to articulate this suffering. This even leads Wilderson to rightfully state that there is an absence of the grammar of suffering. Not only that, but the sentient suspension is also in full intensity to make the faculty of senses, the "structure of feeling" as Wilderson states, to be off balance – say, ossified. This is deliberate, and the anagrammatical inscription is the perverted force that ensures that dehumanization stays intact.

The grammar of suffering with which Wilderson is concerned is the one that confronts the grammar of exploitation and alienation, as these are categories suffered by the worker and not the slave. Exploitation and alienation have remedies that are not extendable to the slave. The grammar of suffering that vexes the slave, argues Wilderson, is one of accumulation and fungibility. Clearly, exploitation and alienation have to do with the suffering of the worker (human) and accumulation and fungibility have to do with the suffering of the slave (non-human). The non-humanity of the slave is based on the very logic of dehumanization. Being fabricated onto property, and subjected to the deathliness of slavery, there is no recourse for the slave. There is no labor question on the table, but the one being having been owned as the result of having one's flesh kidnapped, bought, sold, and exchanged. Wilderson even makes it clear that there are alienated and exploited *beings* and there are accumulated and fungible *things*. The extent of dehumanization makes it more pressing to understand violence not in symbolic and symptomatic terms, but for it to be understood for what it is – structural and gratuitous.

The standing of the human is authorized. The standing of the slave is the opposite. In fact, is there anything standing to that which is dehumanized? If there is such a standing, this will be frowned upon as violence. This is the invitation of elimination. The slave is stood against, and the slave is denied of standing. According to Lewis Gordon (2000), the slave is denied a point of view. This point of view is, for Wilderson (2010), the paradigm of political ontology. It is here that dehumanization is not disavowed but taken seriously as the source of black suffering. This is the suffering of the slave, the one rooted in the deep annals of the eliminationist logic.

Most, at best, the stance is the politics of the slave, the figure who is dehumanized and denied any form of being. The life and death of Aunt Hester is dependent on the will of her master Captain Anthony, who is human after all. The master has the prerogative to lord over the slave. The way of seeing through the eyes of the subject is not the perspective of the slave; but rather, of the subject imposing the world from itself onto the other – the world that crushes the existence of the slave as the non-human who has no place in the world. The world of the human has to do with the way in which the subject sees, and its inscription is the world of the human and for the human. The construction of the coherent embodiment has to do with the subject, and the human question revolves around making the world a better place, and this better place means glossing over the question of enslavement.

Clearly, the question of life as primal has nothing to do with the slave. It is in this discursive code that there is nothing pertaining to the slave. Thus, it will be seen as absurd by the subject to extend its ontological privileges to that which is not human. The slave as the figure of the impossible, is structurally positioned outside the subject with nothing originary and placed as human. Achille Mbembe writes:

> Who is a slave, if not the person who, everywhere and always, possesses life, property, and body as if they were alien things? Possessing life and body as alien things presupposes that they are like external matter to the person who bears them, who serves as their scaffolding. In such a case, the slave's body, life, and work may be attacked. The violence thus perpetrated is not supposed to affect the slave directly, as something real and present. Thus, "slave" is the forename we must give to a man or woman whose body can be degraded, whose life can be mutilated, and whose work and resources can be squandered – with impunity. (Mbembe 2001: 235)

The slave is out there – vulnerable and disposable – the thing that anything and everything can be done to. Thus, as property, the slave is in the firm grip of the master as that which can be destroyed just as the master desires. The slave is stripped of all forms of being, so as to make dehumanization justifiable. The body, psyche, and soul of the slave is sent to wilderness, outside being, outside any place and relationality – hell.

Standing or being relegated outside the capacity to acquire
– what can Aunt Hester acquire that will free her from the
brutality of her master? The affirmation of the constituent
subject has a place in things human and it is the inscription
that instils the discursive code that fixates the binary of
who is human and who is non-human. It is this discursive
code that belongs to Aunt Hester's master as the definer and
chronicler.

The subject acquires the package of existence from the
discursive code, while conversely it extracts life from the
slave. The merciless whipping of Aunt Hester attests to this
and she has no structure to stand on, as there is nothing that
gives validity to her existence. She cannot acquire anything
that is deemed important for the human. The symbolic
practices that have to do with life are for subjects and they
are constituted in the structure. The constitutive subject sees
itself as an individual in the world, and in that, as the subject
of self-mastery. The subject is not reducible to the symbolic
order; the latter is created by the subject. In other words,
there is mutual reinforcement between the subject and the
symbolic order. If both the subject and symbolic order are
in favor of dehumanization, then the brutalization of Aunt
Hester will not call for any moral response or any form of
sanctioning. The subject creates the world, structuring it
through violence and making sense of reality through control
and possession of others. The possession of Aunt Hester by
Captain Anthony compels the slave to see itself as that which
is unseen and non-existent as human.

Taking Aunt Hester's flesh as the point of departure, the
aim is not to resolve anything but to dwell on the inscription
of the flesh. This means wrestling with the question of the
flesh and not the subject. It is only the will of the master that
determines the degree of dehumanization toward the slave.
The lashes that are directed at Aunt Hester's flesh can only
be started, continued, and stopped by Captain Anthony and
not by ethical questions that have to do with the human. It
is clear that no ethical and moral weight can lead to Aunt
Hester's exemption. The suspension of ethics is what Captain
Anthony did and thus confirms that Aunt Hester is nothing

but flesh. Undeniably, what is whipped, under the logic of sentient suspension, is the flesh and not the human being. There is no consequence to this whipping even if Aunt Hester had died. She ceased to exist anyway from the moment of her captivity. What then does it mean to be abstracted and structured as nothing but flesh?

The Flesh

The whipping of Aunt Hester made Douglass come to grips with the abstraction of the human turned flesh. Aunt Hester's whipping is, according to Douglass (1995 [1845]), a "horrible exhibition." What Douglass came to see is the horror of slavery. The beating of Aunt Hester is the way that slavery presented itself to him, and the way he will see himself as the being who is captured and who is waiting for this horror to be directed to him at some point in his life. This "horrible exhibition" as the force that captures Douglass's spectacle is, in itself, the force that structures the logic of the world that he will live in, and the reality has already been framed in line with that horror. It is this "horrible" that should be put squarely into the everyday life of being enslaved and also outside the "event" – that is, its occurrence or not is still a horrible exhibition. Everything stands as a horrible exhibition so long as the figure of the slave exists. To be enslaved is to be subjected to horror, despite its spectrum or degree. Douglass (1995 [1845]: 4) declares: "I never shall forget it whilst I remember anything." It is this event that Douglass saw from the perspective of being a slave and being initiated into the brutality of slavery. Douglass (1995 [1845]: 3) writes: "My first master's name was Anthony." It is from his first master that he saw fleshly designs and the drama-turgy of violence in its realistic materiality. The flesh of the subject is not the flesh of the slave. There is no ontological hyper-visibility and non-corporeality of the subject; that applies only to the slave. The reduction of the slave flesh is not the indictment that faces the subject. The flesh of the slave stands in relation to the thing and there is no human question that comes to being as the human is depleted. The flesh of the thing is non-corporeal because the flesh of Aunt Hester is extracted from her bodily existence as the institution of slavery consumes the flesh.

Aunt Hester is structured by Captain Anthony's will as the master subject. His absolute truth is to be obeyed by Aunt Hester – she should not do what the master does not want. Her whipping is indicative of the fact that Captain Anthony's "Word" should be obeyed at all times. The Word said that Aunt Hester should not go out at night and that she should not be caught in the company of a young slave, Ned/ Edward Roberts, who was paying attention to her. Also, to be known, which is something that underlies this demand for the obedience, is that Captain Anthony was jealously eyeing Aunt Hester. At no point should there be a contravention. It is the Word – the absolute truth, on the wrong side of which Aunt Hester happened to fall by contravening the two orders of the master. Douglass (1969 [1855]: 85) gives the damning account of the primal scene and first, its originary and the impossible command of Captain Anthony.

Later, in his narrative, Douglass gives an account of Aunt Hester, and now she is named Esther. But the originary name, Aunt Hester, will be maintained throughout the text. It is evident that, as J. Kameron Carter (2008) articulates, the name was, as with other names and scenes later, "tweaked" – from Aunt Hester to Esther, from Ned to Edward for instance. What is consistent is Douglass's diagnostics, the critique of the logos of slavery. According to Carter (2008: 295), this "re-registers both the meaning of his aunt's beating and the psychological effect it had on him."

> This was a young woman who possessed that which is ever a curse to the slave-girl; namely – personal beauty. She was tall, well formed, and made a fine appearance. The daughters of Col. Lloyd could scarcely surpass her in personal charms. Esther was courted by Ned Roberts, and he was a fine looking young man, as she was a woman. He was the son of a favourite slave of Col. Lloyd. Some slaveholders would have been glad to promote the marriage of two persons; but, for some reason or other, my old master took it upon himself to break up the growing intimacy

between Esther and Edward. He strictly ordered her to quit the company of said Roberts, telling her that he would punish her severely if he ever found her again in Edward's company. This unnatural and heartless order was, of course, broken. A woman's love is not to be annihilated by the peremptory command of any one, whose breath is in his nostrils. It was impossible to keep Edward and Esther apart. Meet they would, and meet they did. (Douglass 1969 [1855]: 85–86)

The love of Esther for Edwards is justified.

Esther was evidently much attached to Edward, and abhorred – as she had reason to – the tyrannical and base behaviour of her master. Edward was young, and fine looking, and he loved and courted her. He might have been her husband, in the high sense just alluded to; but WHO *was* this old master? His attentions were plainly brutal and selfish, and it was as natural that Esther should loathe him, as that she should love Edward. Abhorred and circumvented as he was, old master, having the power, very easily took revenge. (Douglass 1969 [1855]: 86–87)

What was Aunt Hester's transgression? Daring to love Edward. The encounter with the scene causes Douglass to describe vividly "the blood-stained gate," which is not a metaphor but the real picture of slavery. To enter into this gate is what Douglass equates with hell. Even if that blood can be wiped out or cleaned afterwards to leave the gate spotless, blood is always thicker and will always be there. The sadistic drive of the whip serves as the impulse for the visual orgy – the blood must be there – a spectacle, scopic discipline, and that being spectrality.

I happened to see this exhibition of his rage and cruelty toward Esther. The time selected was singular. It was early in the morning, when all besides was still, and before any of the family, in the house or kitchen, had left their beds. I saw but few of the shocking preliminaries, for the cruel work had begun before I awoke. I was probably awakened by the shrieks and piteous cries of poor Esther. My sleeping place was on the floor of a little, rough closet, which opened into the kitchen; and through the cracks of its unplanned boards, I could distinctly see and hear

what was going on, without being seen by old master. Esther's
wrists were firmly tied, and the twisted rope was fastened to a
strong staple in a heavy wooded joist above, near the fire place.
Here she stood, on a bench, her arms tightly drawn over her
breast. Her back and shoulders were bare to the waist. Behind
her stood old master, with cowskin in hand, preparing his
barbarous work with all manner of harsh, coarse, and tanta-
lizing epithets. The screams of his victim were most piercing.
He was cruelly deliberate, and protracted the torture and as
one who was delighted with the scene. Again and again he drew
the hateful whip through his hand, adjusting it with a view of
dealing the most pain-giving blow. (Douglass 1969 [1855]: 87)

Douglass (1995 [1845]: 4) has this to say: "The louder she
screamed, the harder he whipped; and where the blood ran
faster, there he whipped longest." Douglass (1969 [1855]: 80)
intimates: "Poor Esther has never yet been severely whipped,
and her shoulders were plump and tender. Each blow, vigor-
ously laid on, brought screams as well as blood." This scene
of terror, the one of scream and blood, the two which caused
Captain Anthony to intensify his blows, is the mark of
dehumanization. This was, according to Carter (2008: 292),
"all punctuated with the presence of fast-flowing blood." The
scream and blood of Aunt Hester could not stop the beating.
This even led her to beg, as Douglass (1969 [1855]: 88) writes:
"'Have mercy; Oh! have mercy' she cried; 'I won't do so no
more'; but her piercing cries seemed only to increase his fury.
His answers to them are too blasphemous to be produced
here." Captain Anthony's sadistic drive is marking the flesh
through the whip; the bleeding that results from it, and the
intensification of whipping are pleasurable in that nothing
can stop the whipping. Here is what Douglass (1969 [1855]:
88) says in resolve: "The whole scene, with all its attendants,
was revolting and shocking, to the last degree; and when
the motives of this brutal castigation are considered, has
no power to convey a just sense of its awful criminality."
Carter (2008: 294) adds: "The scene, in other words, allows
Douglass to dramatize an ontology of slavery and the ethical
structure of white articulacy and black inarticulacy." Sharpe
(2010: 9) amplifies: "In other words, this violation, this

being, or being positioned to be, fucked over and across time is freighted with signifying access to a freedom narrative." This, obviously, ties with the absence of the grammar of suffering that Wilderson (2010) explicated earlier in order to understand the incomprehensibility of the violence to which the black is subjected. Certainly, black suffering, to concur with Wilderson, is a phenomenon without analogy. Douglass is not only at the limits of saying something, but at the limits of language itself. This scene, this monstrosity as Sharpe (2010) shows, is the awful configuration through which power, in its perverse forms, sadistically enacts itself as desire, pleasure, and fulfillment, which, then, as domination, robs the tongue of the capacity to speak about what the eyes saw and what the sensorium faculties of the body felt and experienced.

Spillers (2003: 67) evokes what she calls "the hieroglyphics of the flesh" in order to account for Aunt Hester's sadistic brutalization as a result of her contravention of the master's Word. The master's Word, just like the lash of the whip, is what Anthony Farley (2005) refers to as the mark. Just to underline, Farley (2005: 223) writes: "The mark must be made on the flesh because that is where we start from." It is the flesh that determines difference, human hierarchy and, in the account of Aunt Hester, how she cannot be treated as a human being. Alexander Weheliye (2014: 32) calls for ways to "understand the workings of the flesh." This is underpinned by Spillers's revelation of the flesh as the site to be violated at will. Yet, there is no recourse to its irreparability but the continuing of terror exercised upon it through, as Weheliye (2014: 66), states, "*prescribed* internecine degradation." For Spillers (1987), the markings of the flesh signify the entity that is written in blood and a scene of radical expulsion, which shows the nakedness of dehumanization. It is misrecognition and disregard; the whipping of the master as the hieroglyphics of the flesh, the whip being the writing instrument upon the surface that is the flesh and the ink being the blood that comes from ceaseless lashes marked upon Aunt Hester's flesh. What, therefore, emerges is that the body ceases to be as such, the non-corporeal; it is property, a thing. It can be itemized, catalogued, tagged, classified, ordered, priced, sold, and whatever else that can be done to a thing. From capture, birth, inheritance, and transaction, the slave is the property of the master. The flesh, according to Spillers, is the entity that stands as evidence against the high crimes committed against it. Thus, the flesh is the witness. Alas, there is no juridical structure that can listen to its testimony.

Performativity is not the possibility but non-recognition of Aunt Hester's humanity and the look for the ways in which violence veils itself – that is, "the extreme and paradoxical condition of slavery, often mistaken for nonsense or joy" (Hartman 1997: 35). As Farley (2005: 239) amplifies: "The slave is trained to enjoy being taken for an object. The master's will is the slave's desire." This is sadistic; the master extracts at the level of excess to create the nothingness of the slave. If performativity is to be taken into account, it does less to account for the flesh. Aunt Hester cannot be reduced to the mercy of what Hartman refers to as the liberal extension of feelings. In performance there is a captive body. Therefore, the captive body is an oxymoron if performance is introduced as a radical breakdown or some form of freedom drive as Moten claims.

Slaves, according to Hartman, are fundamentally the site of white enjoyment, its excess in order to fulfil whatever degree of the master's fantasy. By striking terror on the slave's flesh, the master extracts enjoyment. It is the flesh that shows the enjoyment of its kind, the one that "whites were allowed a great degree of latitude in regard to uses of the enslaved" (Hartman 1997: 23). To be the slave, as a site of enjoyment, the site of extraction, fundamentally means to be captive. While the master enjoys the slave, there is no joy to the slave but pain, suffering, misery, and all the existential ordeals that negate humanity. Slavery, Hartman (1997: 25) insists, is "observing violence and conflating it with pleasure." This means the pleasure of the master is the erasure of the slave, since the making of the slave is being extracted from humanity. By exercising violence on the slave, the master justifies himself for having committed violence, as the slave is nothing. For the master derives pleasure from dehumanization.

Hartman does not rush to the politics of possibility for the fact that there is a need for a deeper excavation of Aunt Hester's flesh and its non-corporeality. The reproduction of the primal scene is of no help, but it is essential as a discursive device to understand the logic of dehumanization. For this to occur, the scene of subjection and not the scene of objection should be put squarely onto that of dehumanization – to engage in the analytics of the flesh – to unmask the despotic terror.

Among a constellation of questions that Mbembe (2001) puts forth – it is essential to curl a few of which are fundamental in understanding the human question. This is mainly because these are the questions that prove essential to account for Aunt Hester's flesh as the racialized entity, where violence is something that remains attuned to it as something that is beyond restraint and, if such violence is something to be comprehended, it proves to be nothing but horror. Even though sadistic enactments of this violence would be examined, it is important to go to Mbembe (2001: 174), who delivers the series of questions thus: "But what does it mean to do violence to that which is nothing? What is a human being and who is not, and by what authority is such a distinction made?" These questions are essential to understand the figure of the slave, the one who is not a subject, but the figure reduced to flesh. According to Mbembe, the subject exists in the fixture of freedom and bondage. The subject is the human as such, but the one who has her humanity taken away by means of violence, making her nothing and continuing to violate that which is nothing.

It is important to add that this is the subject who is dehumanized in order not to be human or "to be" human, the latter which is not the case, of course. The subject is the human, and a thing is not human. In other words, to do violence to the subject and to do violence to a thing spark difference. If the subject can be accounted for, the fact stems from the subject having ontological weight as the figure of the human. In the event of death, the subject dies and there is mourning that follows. There cannot be mourning for a thing, as it never existed before. The ontological difference remains stark, and this shows the different lived experience between those who dehumanize and those who are dehumanized. The birth of the subject is possible in the realm of the human, and this is the subject that possesses humanity – that is, humanity is born. Things are not born, they are invented (in this case it is violent invention as absolute destruction as that is what dehumanization is) and things are outside humanity as such.

Mbembe's conception of the subject is in relation to its subjection. Both are in close physical contact and violence becomes, as Mbembe (2001: 174) notes, "a labyrinth of forces at work." This violence, Mbembe insists, is saturated into structures and institutions. It is reality as such, and it has the Althusserian dimension as it is enforced by what Mbembe calls persons of the flesh and bone – the *commandement* that is akin to the Repressive State Apparatus. The violence that Mbembe registers is set in the passage where it is easy to get lost – it is, in fact, a galaxy and its multi-folded constellations. To qualify, Mbembe (2001: 175) deploys "the spirit of violence," which "makes violence omnipresent; it is presence – presence not deferred (except occasionally) but spatialized, visible, immediate, sometimes ritualized, sometimes dramatic, very often caricatured." This is what it is, as it is, and how it is pervasive.

The slave is not a usable human, but the object of value – the value accumulated by the master – the slave as nothing at the domain of being human. The exterior of the human is what the slave is – nothing. The master determines the fate of the slave, and this is not in the realm of choice. The slave can be obedient and still be killed by the master; the slave can be complicit and still be killed by the master; and the slave can be rebellious and still be killed by the master. Slaves do not know what satisfies the master, even if they think they do, as their fate is contingent upon knowing that they will die under the brutality of the master anyway. The life of the slave is that of the master. Having no value of their own as being human and having value in terms of their overuse and misuse, deprivation and degradation, shame and humiliation, dehumanization and death, the slave has nothing that counts as human. The slave, Mbembe insists, is deemed by the master to have no reason and transcendence to aspire to. The value of the slave lies in being a tool of the master. The tool of the master is a *thing* and *nothing* at the ontological level. Mbembe writes:

> The "thing" – and, by extension, others, the Other – can be made mine. In this sense, I have ownership of it; I possess it. It can be absorbed in, and by, my *I*. I can submit by myself. I can realize myself at its expense. Thus I create myself as a free, autonomous individual in a class of my own: as a subject. (Mbembe 2001: 19 [emphasis original])

This is the "objective thought" of the master subject, the human in his own right, the individual who relates to the world, his world – the figure who lords over everything that is there in the world. The master subject is the "I" whose objective thought not only justifies himself as human but himself as lord – the individual as the transcendental subject. His existence is that of *I for I* while denying the existence of the other by creating *I and Other*, where dehumanization and death are rendered possible. The ontological justification of the "I" is the master himself, who claims not to need any form of justification because he is justification in himself. The master subject owns a thing that he lords over, the thing is his by virtue of his own justification. This excess of justification is nothing but narcissism. The master subject sees the world from his "objective thought," his thought is not only definitive – it is absolute truth. This is the truth that does not need any form of verification, it is absolute. This absolute truth is not a discursive register, but the being of the master subject himself. Everything that has to do with reality and existence rests with the master himself. Narcissism makes the possibility of boundlessness; everything has it in the "objective thought" – the definer and chronicler of objective truth. It thus remains a dubious fact – that is, the master is the absolute truth and the slave as a thing signifies a lie.

If Aunt Hester's flesh is to be located in this violence, what emerges is the collapse of the narrative that seeks to narrate it. It is the spirit of violence that haunts Aunt Hester's flesh. She is violated because the spirit of violence signifies her to be vulnerable to violence – or, the spirit of violence annihilates her as her flesh is incarcerated. Not only is this at the level of possession, but Aunt Hester is not being allowed to be on her own. She is violated by the structure that makes Captain Anthony her master, the institution that makes her the flesh that is commanded by Captain Anthony's will. The spirit of violence is directed to its referent – Aunt Hester's flesh. This flesh is haunted by the sadistic drive, its impulses, its excess, its perverted fantasies. Why would there be an acute narrative to give account of such madness?

Douglass gives the narration, but he still has no narrative, or the linguistic currency to account for the spirit of violence that befell Aunt Hester. Even though he gives a vivid explanation, it still does not capture the extent or excess of the violence against that which is nothing. For Douglass, Aunt Hester is the subject *qua* human and not a thing. By giving her an elegant description as a woman of note, the spirit of violence that unmakes her as such and makes her as a thing becomes interesting. In other words, what would it have been if Douglass had given the account of Aunt Hester through the register of Mbembe's ontological question – "But what does it mean to do violence to what is nothing?" Clearly, what is fundamental is not violence, but its sadistic proportion, its arbitrariness, its inescapable firm grip, the one that mutes the language that seeks to narrate it, the one that blinds the eye that seeks to see it, the one that deafens the auditory faculties of hearing, the one that is felt even not being affected by it directly. This violence is the spirit, it is not the human spirit, it is the spirit of human suspension, of dehumanization. To see Aunt Hester is not to see the human. Thus, her violation is that of a thing – that is, nothing is violated, there is no violence, nothing happened.

What subtends the flesh is the despotic formation, a structure that determines who is human and who is not. The kick-starting of chattel slavery has meant blackness is liquidated from the ontological scale of humanity. To emphasize, the slave and the human are not the same. For slavery means the ontological destruction of the human. Aunt Hester's characteristics as human do not count; she is reduced to nothing and does not even have her own being. She has no humanity to mark as a reference point. She is the property of her master. Captain Anthony is her lord, he can use her and misuse her in the manner he deems fit. Everything starts and ends with the master.

Spillers shows how this inscription is nothing but violence – topology and topography of terror – the abstraction of the body from its form, which then results in ontological erasure. The flesh signifies, according to Katherine McKittrick (2006: 70), "an empty vessel, a commodity, an unsuffering property." It is clear that this is not the body of the human. Spillers is intimate to the witnessing of Aunt Hester's unimaginable brutalization, and it being assigned to the discursive and ontological register of the body that does not belong. Aunt Hester's body is relegated to what McKittrick calls the "ungeographic," as it belongs nowhere but to the master. It is the body that has no interiority or corporeality – it is the abstracted and extracted entity – the flesh.

The analytics of the flesh are necessary, if not fundamental for understanding Aunt Hester's flesh. The flesh is the site where violence is exercised and where it makes its marks visible. As the flesh of Aunt Hester bears no element of corporeality by virtue of her dehumanization, it being made the entity of extraction and abstraction – the corporeality as the embodiment that is outside being – Aunt Hester is in the domain of nothingness. It is this nothingness that gives Captain Anthony power as the master – that is, *the master is the master* in so far as the slave is nothing. Also, to add, for there to be the master, there must be the invention of the slave. The will of the master being exercised upon the flesh, it is the will without restraint, excessive in proportion and its sadistic drive comes to nothing that is akin to pleasure (perhaps if this pleasure is that of the master alone in which terror is mistaken for pleasure). Spillers (2003: 21) amplifies this when he says that "slavery's technologies are through marking, but also suggest that 'beyond' the violating hand that laid on the stigmata of a recognition that was misrecognition, or the regard that was disregard, there was a *semiosis* of procedure that had enabled such a moment in the first place."

The flesh as the analytic serves as the perspective through which Aunt Hester is looked at. She is not the human; to Captain Anthony's whip she is just the flesh. Of course, the flesh of the human being is taken for granted in that it is the embodied entity. The human is not reduced to the flesh. The flesh is without consideration, as the human is human after all. But to the slave, who has been abstracted and extracted from humanity, there is this radical separation wherein the slave has no access to any ontological faculties of the human. Therefore, what is done to the flesh is not done to the human. The slave lives the life that is not life, a void, a delirium, and nothingness. Aunt Hester finds herself there and this is the life that is determined by Captain Anthony – the master in the capacity *qua* master. Life and death rests in his will, Aunt Hester's life is in his hands; he can let her live or he can kill her the way he deems fit. To be the master is to possess that which is nothing, to do whatever to *it* and to practice any form of what Hartman (1997) terms "terror making," which is the operating logic of the power vested in the master by himself and for himself.

The flesh, according to Hartman (1997: 3), signifies the "slave's ravaged body ... the spectacular character of black suffering." Hartman opens her text with Aunt Hester's brutal whipping and hastens the fact that to be enslaved is to be subjected to "despotic terror." If there is to be subject formation, that does not materialize to the slave as destruction, suppression, erasure, and the slave being nothing but the flesh. For Hartman, to reproduce the brutal account of Aunt Hester is not primacy, as this can be an anesthetized pain and the narratives that reproduce it will go to the banal extent, rendering the pain as the thing to be transcended. The shocking and the horrible, for Hartman, are not essential, as they can create a routinized display of terror (which will not be terror due to the anesthetization that is at work).

Hartman's (1997: 5) intent is to look, among many other things, at the flesh – the "brutal exercise of power upon the captive body rather than ameliorating the chattel condition."

By offering the alternative reading to Hartman, Moten (2003) asserts that there is resistance in the sense that the object has the capacity to resist. If such an object means the slave, for Moten there can be resistance to what dehumanizes slaves and reduces them to flesh. For Hartman, the slave is caught in the scene of subjection and for Moten it is in the scene of objection. Aunt Hester is then an object that engages in the objection to its whipping – Captain Anthony's whip is resisted upon Aunt Hester as the object that resists. Moten is interested in the question of the human – that is, the objection of the object that is objectified by slavery yields the possibility of becoming, being human. This comes through the question of the human as the persistent one; it always resurfaces as objects resist. This is the resistance that breeds possibility. The slave is a subject, according to Moten, the one in possession of possibility and emancipation.

While Hartman moves away from Douglass's "primal scene," Moten insists on its focus. So, the crux of Moten's intervention is reanimating Aunt Hester's whipping. The primal scene, for Moten, cannot be avoided, since such a move is illusionary. Therefore, the primal scene should be reproduced. Moten also insists that there is the possibility of pleasure and pain mixing, the recounting of the primal scene notwithstanding. It seems as though sadistic (non)relations if evoked should be re-examined to determine if it is well-fitting to yield agency. It is important to ask: Is it possible for there to be agency while dehumanization remains intact? Of course, for Moten, dehumanization is not the crux of the "primal scene" in so far as *it is* to Hartman. Moten (2003: 5) formulates some telling questions: "Is there a way to disrupt the totalizing force of the primality Douglass represents? Is there a way to subject the unavoidable model of subjection to a radical breakdown?" These are necessary questions for the problematization of the subject and its becoming – questions that offer possibilities for unraveling the human question; perhaps, to resolve its paradox, to bring answers maybe – or, to insist on the human aspect of the slave and see agency necessary for emancipation.

More fundamentally, however, the opposite of these possibilities faces a deadlock with Aunt Hester's flesh. The contention of the primal scene seems to clearly suggest different registers. On one hand, Moten insists on the primal scene and its radical breakdown because of the capacity of the slave to resist, or to exist; while on the other hand, Hartman refuses the preoccupation with the primal scene for it is the very fact of it being available for reproduction that leads to its anesthetization. Hartman goes straight to the analytics of the flesh and the violent inscriptions to which the flesh is subjected. If performativity is to be taken upon (and not as a focus) perhaps it is important to highlight the following: for Moten there is a possibility of "freedom drive" – the radical force that constitutes the making of the human as such.

Farley (2005: 225) writes: "Bodies are marked white-over-black." It is this marker that justifies mastership – the master as the figure that lords over the slave on the basis of being white. To the slave, the master is the same thing as the slaveholder and the overseer. Both the slaveholder and the overseer assume the same position in relation to the slave – they mean one and the same thing – the master. What the master is known for is the figure that unleashes violence on the slave. Captain Anthony had an overseer by the name of Mr. Plummer, who Douglass vividly describes thus:

> Mr. Plummer was a miserable drunkard, a profane swearer, and a savage monster. He always went armed with a cowskin and a heavy cudgel. I have known him to cut and slash the women's heads so horribly, that even the master would be enraged at his cruelty, and would threaten to whip him if he did not mind himself. (Douglass 1995 [1845]: 3)

Later Douglass would say the following about him:

> This overseer – a Mr. Plummer – was a man like most of his class, little better than a human brute; and, in addition to his general profligacy and repulsive coarseness, the creature was a miserable drunkard. He was, probably employed by my old master, less

on account of the excellence of his services, but for the cheap rate at which they could be obtained. He was not fit to have the management of a drove of mules. (Douglass 1969 [1855])

From the above, it is clear that Mr. Plummer, the overseer, assumed the role of the master and his conduct is as such. As Carter (2008: 292) intimates: "In speaking of Plummer's 'bloody purpose,' Douglass seems to align the overseer Plummer with the biblical figure Cain." Mr. Plummer is informed by homicidal impulses beyond restraint. That is how Douglass (1995 [1845]) described him, and also called him a "savage monster." Even though he knew his place (though he crosses boundaries that "enraged" Captain Anthony), he never ceased to have the place of the master. The threat that he would be whipped by Captain Anthony is just an empty one. If there is something that Captain Anthony enjoys, it is the violent and sadistic character of Mr. Plummer. Douglass attests that Captain Anthony was not a humane slaveholder – as if there is anything like one. Even though Captain Anthony was enraged by the barbarity of Mr. Plummer, all he was worried about was that Mr. Plummer should not impersonate him. But that changed nothing in the desire of Mr. Plummer to be a master. Yes, Mr. Plummer reigned like Captain Anthony. The slaves should not see the hierarchy of mastership – the height of the slaveholder above the overseer.

To quarrel with Douglass, though, is to expect humanness from the slaveholder. Even the extreme degree of benevolence cannot extinguish that of a slaveholder. What needs to be affirmed is that mastership cannot be separated from fleshmongering. The barbarity of Mr. Plummer did not affect Captain Anthony at the humane level. Rather, the place of this affect is at the place of being a master – the cruelty of the overseer should not be exercised more than that of the master. That is what affected Captain Anthony; the barbarity is at that level. There cannot be any feeling of compassion for slaves that Captain Anthony had tasked Mr. Plummer to oversee. Also, to note, Captain Anthony made Mr. Plummer his extension. When the slaves see Mr. Plummer, they actually see Captain Anthony.

Douglass commits an error in making a distinction between two overseers, Mr. Severe and his successor, Mr. Hopkins. Douglass describes Mr. Severe as a cruel man, as his name suggests, Douglass (1995 [1845]) writes: "He seemed to take pleasure in manifesting his fiendish barbarity. Added to his cruelty, he was a profane swearer." Actually, Mr. Severe is the same as Mr. Plummer, both being profane swearers and sadists of note. Douglass even goes on to note that Mr. Severe continued to swear even in his moment of death. Mr. Severe's successor, Mr. Hopkins, was regarded as the opposite of his predecessor. He is said to be less profane, not cruel, even not noisy. Mr. Hopkins as an overseer is the sovereign figure above the slave – he enslaves. Douglass (1995 [1845]: 7) narrates: "He whipped, but seemed not to take pleasure in it. He was called by the slaves a good overseer." This is the error of seeing the good in the evil institution of slavery. Mr. Hopkins is the overseer, he enslaves. The slaves who saw him as good did not want the end of slavery, it seems. This then suggests their contentment with having an overseer who is better than his cruel predecessor. Even though Mr. Hopkins is claimed not to have taken any pleasure in whipping, this might be an error by Douglass. The very act of whipping is pleasure seeking, the one who whips is gratified by consuming the flesh of the slave. The fact that still remains is three-fold with regard to Mr. Plummer and Mr. Hopkins: One, both were overseers and they subjected slaves under the despotic terror of slavery; two, they are the extension of their master by cracking the whip on the flesh of the slaves; and three, they did not see humans, they saw slaves and they solidified dehumanization.

Having stated that Captain Anthony was not a human slaveholder (something that cannot be expected) it is interesting that Douglass gives another twist to Captain Anthony. Douglass writes:

> He was a cruel man, hardened by long years of slaveholding. He would at times seem to take great pleasure in whipping a slave. I have often been awakened at the dawn of day by the most heart-rending shrieks of an own aunt of mine, whom he used

to tie up to a joist, and whip upon her naked back till she was literally covered with blood. No words, no tears, no prayers, from his gory victim, seem to move his iron heart from its bloody purpose. (Douglass 1995 [1845]: 4)

Clearly, Douglass's twist shows how Captain Anthony is not humane. Or, perhaps, it is Aunt Hester's heartless whipping that makes him suspend the "humanness" from the master? At no point, of course, did Douglass claim that Captain Anthony was humane. The contention has to do with the paradox (master + humanness) – that is, contra this fusion, the humane master is an oxymoron. Thus, Captain Anthony did not have to commit this act of whipping Aunt Hester to be disqualified from humanness. The master is not humane by virtue of being a slaveholder. This also includes those who are in support of slavery – there is not selflessness and kindness in slaveholding.

Interpellation and Extraction

For Louis Althusser (1971), the production of the ruling ideology, subjection to the ruling ideology, stems from the institution that produces subjection emanating from the superstructure that produces the infrastructure. The slave falls outside the law, state and ideology. As for the analytics of Althusser, they go so far as to account for the subjection of the subject. The state, which Althusser terms the Repressive State Apparatus, is distant from the subject, unlike the master who is fatally coupled to the slave through intimacies of terror. The slave and the master exist in the same space; Aunt Hester was on Captain Anthony's plantation. In sum, even though the state is the larger corpus of violence, and it cascades down to the everyday life of the subject, the slave is in the possession of the master, and not the state.

No amount of human articulation could save Aunt Hester from being abstracted to the level of nothingness. For she is the slave and the figure that does not ontologically count. Douglass (1995 [1845]: 4) foregoes: "She was a woman of noble form, and of graceful proportions, having very few equals, and fewer superiors, in personal appearance, among the colored or white women of our neighborhood." Despite it all, alas, Aunt Hester is enslaved and that is it. She is not her own, she is captive, she belongs to Captain Anthony.

Aunt Hester as the slave falls outside interpellation. There is no interpellation of the slave but that of the subject. The subject as that which is constitutive cannot be reduced to a thing, as the subject constitutes ontological density, while there is nothing ontological about the thing as *the thing does not exist*. What, then, to make of interpellation? Althusser (1971: 2) writes: "It follows that, in order to exist, every social formation must produce the conditions of its production at the same time as it produces, and in order to be able to produce." What Althusser insists on is production forces and the existing forces of production as sites through which the condition of production materializes. If production happens, it produces the subject and then the subject who assumes the figure of the sovereign can then invent the slave. Production is more about continuity and invention is more about the beginning. Therefore, the human question becomes important in order to think through the ontological configurations that Ruth Gilmore (2002) refers to as fatal couplings of power in order to understand how power produces the subject and how it invents the slave.

Interpellation occurs when individuals are turned into subjects. Althusser (1971) emphasizes that interpellation of individuals as subjects is embedded in ideology, and ideology and interpellation are one and the same thing. Everything operates at the privatized level as opposed to the violence actualized to the slave. Interpellation, as Althusser states, occurs in the example that happens when the police hail at the subject: "Hey you there!" and then the subject looks back without even knowing whether it is the individual at whom the hailing is directed. By the fact of looking back, already the subject has been interpellated. The subject in Althusser's case has a choice of whether to be interpellated or not. Even if the choice remains elusive, Althusserian insistence is that the subject is always interpellated; but still, there is a choice. The slave exists in the denied existence and is structured by dehumanization. The slave does not need to respond to the hailing, as the slave is already captive. The Althusserian subject is human, and Aunt Hester falls outside such an ambit. The violence that is faced by the subject is that of the state apparatus, which is divided into the Repressive State Apparatus and the Ideological State Apparatus, where the state by its extension interpellates subjects. But what about the extraction of the slave from humanity? The slave exists in close proximity to the master and the extension of the master goes to slave overseers, who are masters of their own accord, stretching their unchecked deputized power to be more brutal than the masters themselves. There is no need for hailing, the slave has already committed an offence, and the lashes of the whipped are dispatched onto the flesh just for the sake of doing so. Death lingers and the flesh of the slave has no relational capacity to the master.

The process of constructing the human is based on reason. This serves as the justificatory mechanism through which the intention of the slaves is made to stand as truth. This form of reasoning and justificatory mechanism serves as the mode of signification. Extraction is the manner in which the slave is made to be through the subjective understanding of the master. The slave is there because the master invented the slave, and it is the master who named the slave as such. According to the understanding of the master, the slave is nothing but the slave. This understanding is called abstraction, the reality as created by the master.

Agency seems to be the panacea to all challenges, especially injustices that face the human. Michael Hardt and Antonio Negri (2009) call for the constitutive collectivity of the human in the politics of solidarity, insurgency, militancy, and practices of opposition that give birth to the conception of the multitude, which is the indignation where resistance of power animates itself and thus yields possibilities of expressions of freedom. This is confrontation, stand-off, combat, insurgency, and the multitude as agents that stand against injustice. What is of interest is what Hardt and Negri call

the 'jacquerie,' who expresses double power to confront the
status quo. For this to materialize, the human must assume
the subjectivity of the jacquerie.

> The violence of the jacquerie, on the one hand, overflows
> reasonable measure and destroys the objects of its wrath
> seemingly indiscriminately: think of the tales of white coloni-
> alists killed by revolting slaves in Haiti or the images of
> Detroit in flames during the riots of summer 1967. The sponta-
> neity of the jacquerie, on the other hand, according to the
> standard narrative, leaves behind no organizational structure,
> no legitimate institution that can serve as an alternative to the
> power overthrown. The jacquerie burns out in a flash and is
> gone ... Despite their brevity and discontinuity, the constant
> reappearance of these jacqueries profoundly determines not only
> the mechanism of repression but also the structure of power
> itself. (Hardt and Negri 2009: 237)

The jacquerie stands off against Althusser's state apparatus,
the structure itself, including its auxiliary and extensive
mechanisms of interpellation. The repressive mechanism
is the totality of violence. The jacquerie is the subject that
embodies and expresses agency. The fulfillment would then
be the transformation of the jacquerie into the multitude. This
is the configuration of the subject in what Michel Foucault
(1997) names as the field of power. As the subject that resists,
the jacquerie is always in a network, a loose one so it seems.
As Hardt and Negri (2009: 238) elaborate, "there is always
a pressure to make common the actions of the multitude, and
this organizational initiative most often takes the form of the
construction and the reproduction of informal networks."
The multitude in the field of power assumes a very interesting
character in that they have no interest of taking power but
to dismantle it. The state apparatus is brought to a complete
end.

The anticipation of Hardt and Negri's political project
is the critique of domination and creating another reality.
This reality is the one that Negri and Hardt posit as instituting altermodernity. Both insist on the horizon that comes
through the politics of happiness embodied by laughter.

It is clear that laughter, according to this perspective, is the potent *tour de force* that will institute happiness, thus defying the existential misery of humanity. This laughter, it seems, will even triumph during misery until its very end. The declaration of happiness is the affirmation of the politics of altermodernity.

> In the face of this arrogance of power, the most adequate response, rather than lamenting our poor lot and wallowing in melancholy, is laughter. Laughter, mind you, is a very serious matter. It is not consolation for our weakness but an expression of joy, a sign of our power. (Hardt and Negri 2009: 382)

In the formation of the multitude, or its constitutive and intersubjective modes, the jacquerie is not the slave but the subject. This is the unraced human being, the one who claims totality as the transcendental subject. The jacquerie is the worker and not the slave. The jacquerie as the subject cannot be dehumanized and there is no concern for the slave as the demands of the latter exceed those of the jacquerie – the interpellated subject.

If the question of the human is to be posed to Hardt and Negri, what prevails is the notion that "we are all human" and also suggests that the plight of the human and non-human is the same. The category of the human is the common who belongs to the *polis* – the political community of the "we." The common in the *polis qua* the subject as human needs to qualify, in relation to structure, the configuration of the "we," which suggests the totality of humanity while turning a blind eye to and being mute about the non-human. Of course, the common is the subject in the world and structure – the *polis* – is the site where power resides, is exercised, enforced, and contested. The subject and structure as revolutionary struggle serve as a means of giving a new form of reality in the world – the inauguration of the politics of happiness and its attended laughter will serve as the negation of the misery that has befallen the *polis*. The non-human stands in a different ontological configuration, where the struggle is not for happiness. Aunt Hester's whipping cannot be remedied by happiness and laughter. The world that Aunt

Hester wants as the slave is the one where there should be the resurrection of the human.

For Foucault (1997: 24), the exercise of power is applied to the body as "a political technology of the body which might be read as common history of power relations and object relations." This is plausible for understanding the situation of slavery as such because this power can be arbitrary at times. But what about the power exercised upon the flesh? Clearly, and more fundamentally, the question of the human refuses to hold onto the basis that it cannot account for the flesh. Thus, the ontological fixation of the flesh is not what the human question is preoccupied with. The body that Foucault describes is the body of the subject. This is the body that has a place in the world, and it is where subjection resides in the form of interpellation. The body of the subject is vexed in power relations, and it is the political field – the field of power as Foucault states:

> But the body is also directly involved in a political field, power relations have an immediate hold upon it, they invest it, train it, torture it, force it to carry tasks, to perform ceremonies, to emit signs. This political investment of the body is bound up, in accordance with complex reciprocal relations, with its economic use; it is largely as the force of production that the body is invested with relations of power and domination; but, on the other hand, its constitution as labour power is possible only if it is caught up in a system of subjection (in which need is also a political instrument meticulously prepared, calculated and used); the body becomes a useful force only if it is both a productive body and a subjected body. (Foucault 1997: 26–27)

Even though there might be traces similar to that of slave-holding, Foucault's focus is not on this aspect, and it would be amiss to transpose the subjection of the subject into the subjection of the slave. Subjection takes different forms when dealing with the body of the subject and the flesh of the slave. The subject is interpellated and the slave is extracted. Extraction means that Aunt Hester's ontological ruin signifies the body of irreparability, and the redemptive discourses and fabrications of setting things anew, of transcending or "dealing with" them, are not enough. That which is irreparable is by definition irremediable. Hartman (2002) clearly shows that there is no way of overcoming the injury of slavery due to this irreparability. The assault on Aunt Hester's flesh is with the past, the present, and the future. Extraction is important for punctuating the annals of slavery because it marks captivity, deportation, and death (Hartman 2002).

The body in Foucault is constitutive; it is the body of the interpellated subject. David Marriott (2015) draws attention to the dehumanized body, which is invented in ways that mean it will lose its corporeality. Extraction signifies this body as racialized. Marriott (2015: 163) writes: "It is racism that produces the racialized body." This is not the body of the subject who is in the field of power but, as Douglass notes, it is the body that is in the jaws of slavery. This body is, Marriott insists, made up of phobias, fantasies, and sadistic desires that intensify disfigurement to make dehumanization possible. The being that is outside the configuration of the human cannot be in the field of power. It is only by means of interpellation of the subject that the symbolic form can remain, and not in extraction of the slave, where the flesh is the liability that then justifies the liquidation of humanity through disfigurement.

The slave is not interpellated, the slave is dehumanized through extraction. The liquidation of life means that death is the defining feature of the slave. The subject lives, while the slave is caught in the vectors of sadistic violence and death. The life of the subject can be suspended; the life of the slave is forever liquidated without any form of temporality. The slave is not the index of the human, as dehumanization reigns supreme. Aunt Hester is reduced to flesh, she has no humanity to speak of and she cannot stand against Captain Anthony and the institution of slavery because everything is against her as the slave. As she is seen by the master, she is a site of fabrications, phobias, fantasies, and sadistic violence. The flesh of Aunt Hester through extraction is invented by slavery, it is the brutal institution that is preoccupied by consuming the flesh – on what to do with it, how to misuse

and abuse it and, more fundamentally, how to reduce
humans who are considered to be a radically different
species, to flesh.

Extraction is about abstraction and form, the unjust justification and unreason posing as reason, the ethos of bad
faith that underpins dehumanization. As Gilmore (2002: 16)
testifies: "The violence of abstraction produces all kinds of
fetishes: states, races, normative views of how people fit into
and make places in the world." Extraction is the signification
of the slave as *a thing*. It is the master who signifies what the
slave is. It is through extraction that there is a thing called
the slave. It is the invention of the slave that must attest to
the power of the master. What, then, to make of the power
of the master as fetishized by the master? What is the master
without power? The master is ruinously coupled with power
– say, power equals the master, and the master equals power
– for there to be power there must be the powerless, and the
slave is a case in point. Aunt Hester is outside the configurations of power as she is not the subject. There is no way
that power is used to give the slave agency to get out of this
powerless position since this is what makes the master exist.
If the slave has power, then the master is rendered irrelevant.
The power as exercised by Captain Anthony possesses her
and it presses down vertically over her. For Captain Anthony
to exist as the master, there should be Aunt Hester – the
slave who is made impotent. The impotence of Aunt Hester
is the excess of power of Captain Anthony. That is why the
excess of power goes to sadistic proportions. Power is used,
misused, and abused against Aunt Hester and it is through
extraction that she is radically expelled from humanity. The
power of the master is not exercised to have an ideological
function; it does not hide behind the state, it is visible, it is
a spectacle. The exercise of power is nothing but sadistic
drive, which affirms the power of the master. Extraction,
as the fetish of the master, signifies the absence of limit, the
dramaturgy of power, power in its bastardized form. From
the moment of capture, the slave, who was human before, is
stripped down ontologically to become flesh, the very thing
that is already dead.

On Death

Douglass, the slave, confronted by the ordeal of his aunt, exists to endure the markings that come with the being of the slave. The existence of Aunt Hester is similar to that of Douglass in that both of them are slaves. The slave is property whose transaction – as the thing that is bought and sold/used and misused/humiliated and ruined – is not on the basis of labor but that the slave is available to the master's sadistic whims and the excess of will. This is the master's absolute prerogative, and of course there is no limit. To the master, the slave is what Orlando Patterson (1982) calls "a raw body" that is not hired for labor but to serve as the tool of the master, his mere thing.

> If the master sought to exclude as far as possible all other claims and powers in his slave, it nevertheless remains true that he needs both the recognition and the support of the nonslave member of his community for his assumption of sovereign power over another person. An isolated master faced grave risks. (Patterson 1982: 35)

The master belongs to what Nelson Maldonado-Torres (2008) refers to as "community of masters," the community to which every master pays allegiance. The notion of a community of masters valorizes the master's sovereign power, which is needed to maintain the pathos and self-control that keeps the regime of slavery intact (Maldonado-Torres 2008). In point of fact, the community of masters is a law unto itself; and the law is there to confer upon it the sovereign power and the excess of will that capacitates it to lord over the slave. This takes the form of the infrastructural sentiment that binds the community of masters together – the ethos of death as legitimated by law. The slave exists in the matrix of terror. Anthony Bogues (2010: 72) writes: "However, this terror is often not outside the law but functions inside it and it is given legitimacy as authorized death." This is the figure that cannot be spared: everything is against the slave. The law itself is terror. As Patterson (1982) notes, the slave exists as a socially dead person in that with the encounter with the master, the slave is introduced as non-being. This introduction stems from the community of masters, which signifies master morality (the immoral morality that is) that is then constitutive of slavery, from its beginning, its changing faces, to the present.

What black bodies have ontologically in the infrastructure of racism and its constitutive embodiment – the antiblack world – is the question of death. Obviously, death is inevitable, a fact of life and something that must be accepted. It is the question that has been troubling Benjamin Noys (2002: 51) and it goes like this: "What is the time of death?" This question is important, and yet it is problematic to those for whom death is being institutionalized, normalized, and naturalized. In making an incisive inscription of what is slavery, Farley (2005: 222) writes: "Slavery is the rule of law. And slavery is death." These two inscriptions define the location of Aunt Hester in the mechanics of dehumanization. This is not an alternated position – it is fixity as such – the fact of life as it were, the fact according to the master, life as denied by the master, the rule of law and death as determined by the master. If everything is in favor of Captain Anthony as a master and against the slave, then who is Aunt Hester under the merciless whipping of Captain Anthony? Death becomes predictable to blackness because it is the life that is structured by death. It is not only a fact of life, but the ontological violation with which blackness must survive. Black bodies die because they are not subjects who are qualified to ask the question that Noys (2002) poses. This question seems to be very individualistic, and it is about the subject who is a being-in-the-world and who has a place and a sense of relationality that capacitates life. For those who have been incubated into death, being born in its wrath and who are yet also to be liquidated by it, they have nothing to make in order to access life. The question of the time of death, when it will occur, is right when it applies to the subject. This means that death has its time, unpredictable as it may be, but it is not banal. It is the event and it is inevitable. It is not the death that is deliberate and constitutive through the sovereign violence directed toward the enslaved body, to bodies that suffer from uncertainty about when they will die from the intentioned death that cannot be accounted for. Therefore, the intention of having the slave collapses Noys's question "What is the time of death?" Noys's question is temporal in that death is reducible to a particular time. This, in relation to the slave, is problematic in three senses, even though there is the insistence that "we live our lives *within a time of death*" (Noys 2002: 52 [emphasis original]). First, the subject lives and the slave is structured by death. Second, the time of death is every day of the slave, the figure that is outside time. And third, by invoking "we" Noys refers to the subject and not the figure of the black – the slave. Even if the subject suffers ontological violence, this is on the basis of temporality and the event – the time of death. It also means that there was a human before and the human will be restored after the lapse of the temporal and the passing of the event. There is no ontological recourse or reparations on the slave. The subject with which Noys is concerned lived and its existence is not structured by death. The politicization of death, as Noys calls it, does not deal with the death that structures the slave.

Death is qualified, obviously as it may be – as the event and fact of life. But what kind of death, and what does death mean? The death that has been legitimated by subjection, this death as an eventuality can also be questioned in that what will it be called if it is the everyday life – the life that is sanctioned, questioned, litigated, and structured by death. What kind of life is lived if death pervades everyday life? The question of death, as it has been articulated above, cannot be divorced from that of property, its dispossession and privilege as sites that produce death. The degree of violence that affects blackness is the dispossession, a symbol, material, and also, ontological. The slave, as the excluded figure, is put into its own domain – death. Therefore, the ontological erasure that manifests in Aunt Hester's flesh is death. The life of Aunt Hester is linked to the dispossession of life itself; it still remains death. Death is brought to be highlighted because of dispossession, which creates the death-bound subject, and which, according to Abdul JanMohamed (2005:

2) refers to "the subject who is formed, from infancy on, by the immanent and ubiquitous threat of death."

If the shift that Noys (2002) makes – from politics to ontology, from ontology to politics – is to be considered, this is the move that collapses when the slave comes into being. To be structured by death, to not have any form of meaning, to be dead by being marked by death raises serious ontologico-existential questions. Slavery is the domain of death. The very structure of death means that the enslaved is isolated from the world. Slavery is the visual, sensory, psychic, spiritual, and bodily exclusion. Those who embody enslavement and blackness are not ghosts, they are living beings who are wedded to death, and they live in the shadow of death. What is the time of death? Noys is posing the question that can be extended in JanMohamed's death-bound subject thus: What is the time of death for the death-bound subject? The subject and death, and blackness and death have distinctive ontological trajectories. So, JanMohamed's question accounts for blackness and it is distinct from Noys's. "What happens to the 'life' of a subject who grows up under the threat of death, a threat that is constant yet unpredictable? How does that threat permeate the subject's life?" (JanMohamed 2005: 2).

The threat of death is the weight that incapacitates the slave. The master strikes terror in order to heighten and solidify his domination by means of "the threat of withholding the possibility of life and withholding the recognition of the slave as human" (JanMohamed 2005: 267). It is with hesitation, therefore, that the slave should be recognized as human since the master makes the ontological distinction. The logic of dehumanization makes the slave nothing, and this justifies death. It is in enslavement that no ontological metamorphosis occurs, as the slave remains the slave; the figure that is under the will of the master. The life of the slave is the life that is already being taken. Thus, the threat of death and actualization of death remain elusive. Both these logics of death are unjust justifications and, in their final determination, they render the slave as that which is already dead – the slave as the figure of the outside, which represents the figure that contaminates humanity and its dehumanization as being nothing but just. The threat of death and actualization of death, as JanMohamed shows, is nothing but death itself. To mark the collapse of the two is to understand the ways in which the slave cannot make claims or have the starting point of being human while being dehumanized.

Maybe, then, it is important to ask: What does it mean to kill the subject and what does it mean, fundamentally, to kill the slave? By taking into account the ontological distinction between the human and the non-human, then it means that death is temporality to the subject, and it can also be the event. Death to blackness is a given. That is why there is no accounting for blackness in death. The will of the master prevails, and it is the matter of the *when* – that is, when will the slave live and when will the slave die. So, the fate of the black is the fate of the when. This is determined outside the will of the slave and there is nothing such as the will of the slave since existence is denied. There is no concession made to the slave as this is the figure of non-existence. The slave is *the thing of the master*.

By seeing slavery as unjust, Douglass's refusal to succumb to fear and the fear of death, to be exact, does not mean the transcendental potentiality that Noys posits about the shift of politics to ontology. Instead, it is the confrontation of the fear of death. It means, therefore, that politics becomes the very basis of critique and not being in the exclusive mode of ontology, where blackness is haunted by death. Thus, it is death that was suppressed to incapacitate Aunt Hester's politics and render her mute in order not to critique property. The struggle, also, is about the ontology of whiteness, as this is the ontology that produces death. This ontology, by means of white property is the one of privilege. It then means that the slave is caught with the ontology that is corrupt in that it is the one that finds its existence through dehumanization. Therefore, politics and ontology at the realm of property remain non-dependent upon one another. It means, then, that there must be the ontological destruction upon which property is contingent.

Édouard Glissant (1997) evokes the figure of the boat, which puts black bodies in a "nonworld." This is the abyss; it is nowhere because being in the throes of death means living in death. If there is anything to go by, or fate perhaps, death is a fact of life, but to the slave this has been overstretched. The form of death that befalls the slave is not a natural one, but it is a determined fact. It is this determination that continues to mark blackness in death and, as such, this is the legitimation of black invisibility. That which is invisible has no capacity for being there by virtue of its being nothing but invisibility itself. This is not the self-constructed invisibility because slaves are put to death in order not to be visible as humans. What emerges from Glissant is the call for the livable world. This world is constructed in exclusionary terms: it is the world *without*, the world that has nothing to do with the slave and there is no way that the slave, to invoke Glissant, can be the totality of the world through poetics of relation. Glissant (1997: 6) writes: "This boat is a womb, a womb abyss." Glissant is making the instalment of the infrastructure of death that is the existential condition that fortifies slavery. What is being exposed is death in its making and inner workings. Glissant (1997: 6) also insists: "This boat: pregnant with as many dead as living under sentence of death." Clearly, from JanMohamed (2005), it is worthy to ask: Who is this if not the figure of the death-bound subject?

Where is the place of the slave in the world that continuously dehumanizes the slave? While the slave is *marked*, the master is *assigned*. The distinction is imperative, the way life unfolds and thus has different outcomes for the slave and the master, is something that is determined by the latter. To be marked, as Aunt Hester is, to be surveilled and tortured, is the prerogative of the master. Captain Anthony, by virtue of having sovereign power as the master, has been assigned to mark Aunt Hester – the slave. There is no relation between the marked and the assigned. What exists is non-relation. The marked is outside and the assigned is inside of life. To be marked is to be dispossessed. Yet, on the contrary, being assigned is the mode of inscription that proffers entitlement to possess, own, and kill.

The body of the slave is in the clutches of death; it is the being outside the subject as the subject can be deformed and de-subjectivated, but this remains reversible. The subject can be turned into an object, and the object can reconstitute itself in order to become the subject. But, when it comes to the slave, a thing, there is no moment of becoming the subject. The axis of subject–object has nothing to do with the slave and death. The stakes are high on the axis of subject–thing non-relation, but these stakes do not mean that the slave matters. The notion of the death-bound subject cannot be flirted with when it comes to the slave if the slave is a thing. That is unless if Giorgio Agamben (1998) with his concept of bare life is seen as appropriate in understanding the ontological ordeal of the slave. Agamben makes it clear that the *homo sacer* is the figure that is caught in inclusion-as-exclusion, the subject that can be killed but not sacrificed. As it were, it cannot be denied that the *homo sacer* can be in the clutches of death. What is fundamental, however, is to point out that the *homo sacer* is not Aunt Hester, the figure that is reduced to a thing – a mere flesh. So, by extension, the death-bound subject is the subject who lived before. There cannot be a negotiation of the death contract as JanMohamed (2005) states. What is of interest then is that, as JanMohamed says, this is the contract of the master and the slave. To break the contract, the slave chooses death rather than to live in bondage, which is nothing but a suspended death sentence.

JanMohamed's work is key to examine Aunt Hester's dehumanization by Captain Anthony. If JanMohamed's conception of the slave as having undergone subject formation to be a slave or to the death-bound subject is correct, then there are problems that lie ahead. JanMohamed (2005: 267) writes: "The slave's road to freedom lies not through a commitment to work but through the renegotiation of the death contract that has bound him [*sic*] in the very process of forming him [*sic*] as a subject." But it is important first to acknowledge JanMohamed's scepticism of the politics of recognition coming from the labor of the slave. Furthermore, the anti-Hegelian move he makes is pertinent for showing systematically how the slave is dehumanized.

Perhaps it is pertinent to quarrel over two concepts as they relate to the slave. These concepts are the subject and also the death contract. The subject is legitimated to enter into a death contract. This is a matter of choice, something that the subject has. The subject can choose to enter into a death contract or not. What then for the slave, the figure of being who is not a subject? The slave has no choice; the life of the slave is structurally dead, as the slave is in the dead non-relation ontologico-existential condition. There are no terms of engagement or terms and conditions that are contractually inscribed. Even if the contract has binding effects – having signed it and agreed to its terms – the slave is already dead. In other words, those who enter into the contract do so out of choice. JanMohamed (2005: 278) writes: "The economy instituted by the death contract, it must be emphasized, is renewed on a daily basis because the slave must be continually coerced in order for him [*sic*] to 'agree' to abide by the horrifying terms of the contracts." It is clear from this assertion what the death contract signifies, and, by its extension, which is arbitrary, it stands for indebtedness and cannot be nullified. It is the contract that still stands. But then, how is it a contract if those who are party to it include the master and the slave? How is it possible to have a contract between the figure that is alive and the one that is dead? Even though the contract can be coerced through the threat of death how is it then that it stands as a contract? Perhaps that contract can be legitimated as a contract, but the thing is that it cannot be renegotiated. For its terms are the ones that determine the death of the slave through the arbitrary will of the master. The will of the master is articulated outside the contract on the basis of the absence of restrictions. The will of the master is excess and, as such, everything stands against the slave. For there to be a contract or even a death contract, it means that the slave should cease to exist.

What lies in death is the will of the slave. It is the will that comes out of consciousness and the radical pursuit of life as such. The slave narrative as politico-ontological critique serves as testimony to the death that structures the life of blackness. More shows how Douglass seized his freedom to confront the fear that engulfed him by fighting with his master Covey to the point of defeating him. This might be seen as a deadly offense, where the slave stands up to the master. Rather, this should be understood as the politics that confront fear. The slave should have a higher form of consciousness, and that means that the slave should rebel to exist. JanMohamed (2005: 280) insists: "When a slave realizes the truth of this, as many clearly did, then he begins to put himself in a position from which he can renegotiate the death contract." But, yet still, the challenge remains – why should the slave renegotiate the death contract? Why is it that the death contract, which has never been there in the first place, should be renegotiated? Is it not that the terms of the master are not contractual at all? Key to note is that JanMohamed looks at the death contract from two epistemic registers, namely: the political economy (labor power) and phenomenology (potentiality). What still stands though as a matter of critique, the scandalous effect of death as a given to the slave and its acknowledgment of it by the slave, does not suggest that the potentiality of death is the will of the slave. The slave is a socially dead figure of non-relation, who has no power to be present in contractual terms.

The subject, JanMohamed rightfully argues, must agree consciously or unconsciously to become a dead subject with no possibility of self-reconstitution. The subject, and not the slave, can enter into a death contract, abide by its terms, renegotiate it and, in order to be free, can manage as JanMohamed (2005: 2) states, to "break the death contract." The slave has no contractual currency, as there is no choice about agreeing or disagreeing to the will of the master, the dictator of contractual terms, the one who has the last say on what is truth and lies, the arbitrary figure of the sovereign with his exaggerated lordship, the definer and chronicler of the slave's life. The contract is the master because it revolves around the master alone. In the master–slave asymmetrical dead non-relation, to agree or disagree is not material, as the death contract is an oxymoron. Everything is predetermined and set against the slave.

Aunt Hester, being the slave, has no death contract with Captain Anthony as she is already outside contractual currency. Everything is against her; no truth, moral standing, or factuality will count in her favor. Even if it were to happen that the terms of the death contract were favorable to the slave, this would not assist in anything as the master can collapse the contractual terms at will. There is no choice for Aunt Hester. There is choiceless choice where there is nothing better to choose and nothing else to choose. There is no possibility of changing the conditions or dictating terms. There is no transaction, there is no relation, there are no subjects and there is no life. The master and the slave are there, and if this remains as such, there cannot be any form of death contract. JanMohamed is right to state that the slave should control the punctuation mark of the syntax of life by defining the meaning of such syntax. This is only possible if there is no contract, only the antagonistic relation of ending the slave and the master.

Death remains the main protector of master. Death is a tool that possesses the slave. The master invented the slave. The master is not the master in the absence of the slave. For the master to exist as the figure of the sovereign there must be the institution of slavery that is informed by the logic of death. The place that death assumes in the figure of the slave is to be understood not in terms of the violence that is experienced by Aunt Hester and Douglass's traumatic witnessing of it. Rather, death is the slave at the point of invention. The beginning of enslavement is the inauguration of death, the absolute liquidation of being human. The instalment of dehumanization as the reigning code that is propelled by the master prevents all forms of life and creates the life of the selected human – the master as the sovereign subject – the occluded dimension of what is human being nothing but death. If the human is the master, only the master should live. The kick-starting of slavery is death at the moment of capture, the human who is captured ceases to be a human being.

If the slave is property, it means that the slave is a dead thing, as it is the property that has no value. It is the absolute possession of the master as a tool. It is a thing that is owned by the master and the master reigns supreme in it. Why? The master is the master by virtue of dehumanizing the slave. This is unjust justification, but it reigns supreme as it is based on the logic of racism. Aunt Hester is the slave of Captain Anthony; she is a non-being that belongs to the reign of the human. Aunt Hester, it seems, therefore, never existed as human because her ontological configuration is that of total ontological collapse. Death as an ontological marker bans the slave from the constitutive basis of being human. The body, mind, and soul of the slave belong to the master, and this means that they do not have the status of the living but rather the dead, property as such. Property is a dead thing in the ontological sense. Property is subject to use and misuse by the master by his own will. So, Aunt Hester, a captive thing that belongs to Captain Anthony, is the dead human.

Aunt Hester's flesh does not signify the individual or the event, but the totality of slavery and its aftermath. The human question, its ethical dimension and legality, faces difficulty when the figure of the slave is introduced. The slave is not the subject and is not the figure that is related to the world. The paradigm of difference is the one that renders Aunt Hester to be nothing but flesh, as she is ontologically nothing. Aunt Hester's flesh is outside the liberal discursive register of "we are all human" by virtue of its location in the question of slavery as the basis of critique. There is no humanity if there is still slavery and its aftermath. There is no humanity if race is still the organizing principle of the modern colonial world. There is no humanity if the infra-structure of antiblackness still exists. There is no humanity if the despotic terror of blackness still persists. There is no humanity if structural violence and mass incarceration are still the markers of blackness. There is no humanity if blackness is still dehumanized.

To pose questions from the site of being dehumanized has nothing to do with the claim of being human, but every-thing to do with ending dehumanization. Aunt Hester's flesh cannot be seen as that which is violated by Captain Anthony, but as that of being a conduit through which the structural position of being blackened in the antiblack world inscribes, legitimizes, and validates itself. In point of fact, Aunt Hester appears in order to be available for dehumanization. So, her presence in the ontological realm is superfluous as she is the slave. The slave is at the level of disappearance from being human. What does it mean to be the human? This question seems difficult to answer at this moment. Aunt Hester is not human, and her structural positionality as the slave renders the question flat, as it does not correspond with her existential misery. Aunt Hester is flesh, she is the captive figure, and her life is not her own. The human question will be relevant after the infrastructure of dehumanization ceases to exist. This is not the effort of the master, or his generosity. Rather, the revivification of the slave from dehumanization and meaningful creation of the human world will bring other ontological possibilities. Aunt Hester's flesh serves as the cartography of this revivification.

2

The Specter of the Africanistic Presence

It is here where race is the central subject, which Toni Morrison brings to the fore, and thus foregrounds it in the sphere where its matters cannot be left untouched. No territory will remain uncharted. At the center of this intervention is the question of the episteme, which is often presented as a singularity that has nothing to do with race. To think about and through Morrison's episteme is to think about what knowledges are there, and how they have not been accounted for. This is key to grappling with the way blackness, in what she calls Africanistic presence, remains the site that is worth engaging, in that it is the ontological fold that is left unsaid. This is happening also by way of allowing it; this is to be amid silence.

To argue for Morrison's episteme is not to argue not for knowledge as the phenomenon that has nothing to do with being in the racialized world. The being of the black, the being that is denied knowledge, but being itself, brings to the surface ways in which to approach Morrison's episteme. This means, in a sense, looking at the ways of thinking, knowing, and doing blackness, which cannot be erased from the face of existence. This does not mean that there must be "inclusion," but it shows how the canonical formation has been deliberately erasing blackness and creating ways in which blacks are cast as the aberration of knowledge and as being with lacks and deficits. The exposé is clear in this intervention that the black is in, thus in the Africanistic presence, rewriting is the embattled cry.

It is from this conviction that Morrison's Africanistic presence is an important task that confronts the erasure of blackness in the world of letters. In a sense, it can be emphatically said that she exposes the ontological scandal. The scandal that Morrison exposes comes from her work as the investigator and interrogator; blackness being the critical site that confronts the colonial/racist imagination. Morrison is not up to conjuring. She bears witness and then gives a damning account of the black condition. That is why she unmasks what has been hidden and lays bare the truth. The presence of the black does not rest in validating the claim, but it turns to the obvious, which is that there is no way that the black could not be there while being there. The systematic ontological erasure of the black has created a condition that Morrison has engaged in a form of spectrality. This is what the Africanistic presence is, the very concern that will form the basis of this intervention.

On Epistemic Violence

By way of Morrison (1992), her combat against imperial episteme, her meditations create not only writing the self, but the bodily self that accentuates Africanistic presence. Dehumanization is faced with an embattled cry that cannot be interdicted. This cry emanates from the forces of blackness that cannot be tamed and contained. Epistemic violence by means of silencing, distortion, erasure, censor, and absolute denial of the subjectivity of the black is not something that can be pointed out but something that shows how voices of narratives muttering 'this black' are not reducible to the literary affair but give the structure that is tied to the bodily being of blackness.

Since Morrison engages in the rewriting of knowledge, this is not a form of revisionism or historicism. Instead, it is the spectrality of the present. This is where the past and future are not far and between, but rather, entangled. The things that Morrison deals with, like reality, have to do with the contained question of Africanistic presence. By assuming the position of critique on the literary imagination of whiteness, with regard to the question of knowledge, she shows how this has been used for producing and pressing injustice. The combat she launches against the scheme of things is not critique at the level of evaluating the object of knowledge but rewriting it all together. This form of inscription comes back to a more fundamental point, where the question is: What does it mean to rewrite the episteme in the face and belly of epistemic racism? Rewriting the episteme in the line of this question means that Morrison's episteme is the literary and literal combat that (re)imagines other ways of black subjectivity.

The principle of rewriting the episteme is not a totalizing affair with its ambition of becoming universal in application. Rather, the episteme as rewritten by the black must exorcise the colonial demons and confront dehumanization. It is here that the black world departs, as the sole undertaking of the black, of its matters that have to do with knowledge, in the terms set by the black. The black is there to compare, draw, exchange, and dialogue with other discursive practices that depart from where they came. The black refuses to be object of knowledge, a thing just to be studied and having nothing to do except be observed, experimented on, examined, extracted, and "understood." Figuring out the black has been in embedded formation in Western discourse. To this effect, it is worth paying attention to Nahum Chandler's lucid intervention, which attests to the inscriptive critique of the Africanistic bent:

> What this critique seems unable to recognize is that there is not now nor has there ever been a free zone or quiet place from which the discourse of Africanist scholars would issue. Such discourse always emerges in a context and is both a response and a call. It emerges in a cacophony of enunciations that marks the inception of discourses of the "African" and the "Negro" in the modern period in the 16th century. At the

core of this cacophony was a question about identity. On the surface, its proclaimed face, it was a discourse about the status of the Negro (political, legal, moral, philosophical, literary, theological, etc.) subject. On its other and hidden face, the presumptive answer to which served as a ground, organizing in a hierarchy the schema of this discourse, and determining the elaboration of this general question, was a question about the status of the European (and subsequently "White") subject. This hidden surface, along with the exposed surface of a question about "Negro" identity, must be continually desedimented, scrutinized and reconfigured. It is the status of this latter identity or the system that it supposedly inaugurates that is so often assumed in the de-essentializing projects currently afoot in African American and African Diasporic Studies. Or, if this white subject or the system presumed to originate with it is not simply assumed, the necessity, rigor, patience and fecundity of antecedent Africanist discourses as they have negotiated a certain *economy* within which Africanist discourses (antecedent and contemporary, Diasporic and continental) function are too easily diminished, if not outright denied, in this critique. (Chandler 1996: 79–80)

The problematic of purity is what Chandler contends with, so does Morrison – that is, the Africanistic presence is not its valorization. In this formulation, it needs to be stated that the idea of race is not disavowed. It is recentered and problematized, and the critique of racism, by Morrison in particular, is emphasized. Therefore, the operative of the Africanistic presence is not only philosophical, but also the episteme in its broader sense, a standpoint of being.

The way Morrison locates the black is the very practice that opens a set of questions that have to do with the manner in which the black writes itself and how this writing should be couched in liberatory ends that reconfigure the whole field of knowledge.

By being denied existence and then also being erased from the field of knowledge, the black engages in matters that do not violate opposition of this negating force, but rather espouse what the negation is – antiblack racism. That is why rewriting the episteme is inseparable from a critical project of making forceful arguments and a clear standpoint against epistemic racism. It is the problematic that makes the effort of rewriting the episteme not as a way of replacing one hierarchy with the other. Rather, it is the vitalism that is necessary to repair the wreckage of being by taking the world to task with its imperial *mythos* and *logos*, which have entrenched themselves into truth and reality, that is static. If there are debates, differences, or many forms of falsifications, the project that Morrison presents has a different agenda, whose task is to undo everything by being concerned with the problematic of the African presence; the presence that has been denied and excluded from the field of knowledge. The present that is engaged, the problematic mode of inquiry, is moving to another direction opposed to that of enclosure, so as to reconfigure the world from the standpoint of the black as the racialized subject.

The presence of those who are not there, who are not supposed to be there, and who are made to be radically absent, presents the existential absurdity that can be found in the meaning of the problematic presence – that is, Africanistic presence. The epistemic intent, articulation, and expression – authorship as it were – is marshaled with clarity and this is infused with the ethos of Morrison's episteme, which translates itself into practice, standpoint, and everything she stands for and against. Consciously and unconsciously, the Africanistic presence is what the colonial/racist imagination deals with. Consciously or unconsciously, the erasure of the Africanistic presence is the way of its paradoxical presence. It is the presence that cannot be denied in any form. The Africanistic presence is denied by way of perpetuating the thinking of its erasure and elimination. Morrison is concerned with the unacknowledged presence, the presence denied, what is claimed as that which has never been there. The black lived experience is so profound. It knows no amount of erasure or decimation, which, in turn, will render it non-existent. It is there, the ensuring presence.

I want to draw a map, so to speak, of a critical geography and use that map to open as much space for discovering, intellectual adventure, and close exploration as did the original charting of the New World – without the mandate for conquest. I intent to outline an attractive, fruitful, and provocative critical project, unencumbered by dreams of subversion or rallying gestures at fortress walls. (Morrison 1992: 2)

This is a declaration, a bold one at that, setting out the path, the cartographic inscription of how to navigate an antiblack world and this leads Morrison (1992: 3) to continue thus: "In that capacity I have to place enormous trust in my ability to imagine [what] others may represent for me." It is this world that is "wholly racialized" as Morrison shows and, through its antiblackness, the making of the black self is not only the ontological project, but the epistemic one too. The work that becomes the signification of Morrison's existence and the subject/object of her episteme is through writing. This goes beyond the sign, but it is the locus of the politics of existence proper. The lived experience of the black is made legible, and its intelligibility lies with the work of writing. This is a way of creating being, the experiment that Morrison tirelessly conducts. "For them, as for me, imagining is not merely looking or looking at; nor is it taking oneself intact into the other. It is, for the purpose of the work, *becoming*" (Morrison 1992: 4 [emphasis original]). The making of the sense is what the Africanistic presence is. It is the self that has been denied of its selfhood, humanity, and every essence attached to existence writ large. Therefore, by embodying politics, this work is of becoming, and leads Morrison (1992: 4) to further write: "My project rises from delight, not disappointment." Surely, writerly combat comes into being and this is the epistemic project. The making of the self is not to be taken in an abstract sense. Morrison concretizes this by being invested in ways of confronting the mythology-turned-reality that insists that the imperial episteme is universal, and it is knowledge in the absolute sense, thus unparalleled (indeed, dubious at best, if not downright deceitful). What has instituted and constituted knowledge has been the Africanistic presence, which is always rendered absent by the imperial episteme. The investment of this way of absenting has been a cause for concern. Thus, assuming the epistemic position, laying out the terms of engagement, how to be free, and what this freedom means as an imperative, is Morrison's concern. Also, the world that she is in, the one that is predicated by the refusal of blackness, is the world that she dissects in its structured denial because that is not the natural condition, but a colonially racist fabrication that naturalizes the absence of blackness even in its overwhelming presence.

The absolute law is brought into place, by a commandment even, that there is knowledge whose canon is that altar to be worshipped at. By stepping on this altar, kneeling, and submitting on it, that is the higher form of knowledge. Nowhere else should there be knowledge away from the originary point of its canon, its "foundation proper," it is assumed. Put differently, its founding fathers (white dead men of the Euro-North-American *geopolis*) are its gods, and this is disguised as a canon or the paradigm of founding fathers. The body of texts, being declared as such by Morrison (2019: 162), their "definitions reflect on eternal, universal, and transcending paradigm or whether they constitute a disguise for a temporal, political, and cultural specific program." The "battle plain," says Morrison, is the imprinting of dominant texts and others that are written outside of what could be writerliness itself.

The episteme that challenges foreclosure is what is set in motion. Here is Morrison (1992: 10): "To notice is to recognize an already discredited difference. To enforce its invisibility through silence is to allow the black body a shadowless participation in the dominant cultural body." For the black body to stand out (not to be counted as the structure of incorporation and silencing) but to be a bane of the status quo. What is important is to set things in motion by means of unraveling what has claimed to be immune and what should remain unshaken.

From where the black is in relation to the Africanistic presence, and in charting the terms that find a path to this elsewhere, it does not mean that antiblackness will not continue to affect the black. What is the key to remark is, according to Sarah Cervenak (2006), a movement that goes in various directions by opening many paths, and that is the rupturous force. This, as Cervenak (2006: 115) states, is a "movement, itinerant without fixed or localizable social position." The production of the episteme ruptures and lays the foundation and possibilities of elsewhere, where the ideas, forms, and definitions that Cervenak (2006: 116) rightfully articulates are "interstices of materiality and immateriality, presence and absence, form and formlessness, purpose and purposeless and continuum to shape as expression of Blackness, of black life and (absent) presence in the United States." This adds to other geographies, where the humanity of the black is still put into question – ontological absenting/absence writ large. The Africanistic presence composes itself from the word go with an attitude of "an anti-incarceratory drive," which Cervenak (2006: 116) describes as being "articulated as a resistance to the pseudorational, categorical enumeration and valuations by others."

The Africanistic presence, as a way of cultivating the art of existence (even existing otherwise and through the attitude of the elsewhere), clearly means that the cultivation of life is happening in the face of being denied such a life. The black, in the realm of artists, the vanguard formation in articulating and cultivating alternative forms of existence, creates the world that is necessary to come into being. This is what Morrison (2019: 82) says: "Without the full participation of these artists, the focus misleads viewers toward sentimental and caricatured representations of black life as criminal, impoverished, exclusively sensual." Clearly, there is absence of the black in all accounts and, much more pronounced, is what is absent between the earlobes of the black. This pathologization of the black, having nothing substantial in terms of thought, and being reducible to the negativity of primitivism and its epithets, stereotypes, and all forms of denigration, is posed as the justification that there is nothing that can be knowledge. Therefore, the Africanistic presence is the pathologization of absence – nothingness of being. If there is a claim to knowledge or articulation of statements of knowledge being asserted in order to define the dehumanization of the imperial episteme, there is a slight-of-hand dismissal, a criticism that does not put itself forward to be the analytics of the episteme itself. It is as if the pathologization of the black is just a naturalized phenomenon. Put simply, the pathological nature of the black cannot correlate with knowledge.

This is not the claiming of presence as inherently ontological and epistemological, in that what the black is, in the face of the world that denies humanity, is the phenomenon of absence. Being there, present as it were, is being subjected to structural erasure. The humanity and knowledge of the black is relegated to "those who do not exist." Morrison (2019: 143) asks: "How does utterance arrange itself where it has to imagine an Africanist Other?" The utterance that comes from a racialized position and that laments over racial violence and all forms of injustice that knowledge hides, is deemed to be a deliberation that is not constructive or fruitful. There should be no emphasis or mention of identity. If Africanistic presence is mobilized as the locus and point of departure, it gets labeled as parochial, essentialist, divisive, and sordidly racist. What is propagated as the norm, as commonsense, is that race must be transcended. Race is what should not be the issue in the episteme, it is the thing of the past and it should be laid to rest. Say, archaic and offering nothing in the present. There goes this banal logic under the guise of knowledge in its absolute sense. Writes Linda Alcoff (2010: 126): "Identity-transcendence is the epistemic norm." The enforcing of this norm has meant that when the black speaks from the locus of having been violated by the antiblack world, the weight of condemnation follows. It means that the black, as a racialized figure, the racialized that comes from the logic of the imperial episteme, which regards itself as being free from racialization, can do so without eliciting a form of any response that comes from the racialized figure. When those who are racialized articulate their lived experience and critique that racist reality, they get vilified and they, by absurdity if not silliness of antiblackness, are regarded as racist. What Alcoff (2010: 124) calls "epistemic platitudes" are structures that condition the status quo as worthy to be preserved. What is called for, banally so, is for the black to speak "from a position of neutrality and color-blindness" (Alcoff 2010: 124). According to this position, which Alcoff opposes, knowledge is free, and it has no bearing on the lived experience. This liberal consensus has descended as common-sense and those who veer off from its disciplining linearity and take alternative routes are those deemed to be outside the narrative structures of reality. As such, they are branded as being in violation of that reality.

The writerly attendance to the Africanistic presence is, according to Morrison (2019: 97): "articulating that unspeakable part of American history." It is this literary utterance, as Morrison would call it, whose literal and figurative inscriptions are the articulation under duress; strained, distressed, but never constrained, and contained. It is the risky speech, and its expression is necessary, despite the consequence, it is expressed anyway because the struggle is the will not to say something, but to exist for something that is being said. The spirit of complicity is encouraged and instilled. There should be no form of resistance. The status quo should remain and prevail. The weight of silence, which is to say the weight of commandment, spreads "apathy, disgust, resignation, or a kind of inner vacuum" (Morrison 2019: 97). This is the condition that prolongs and deepens pathologization. It is as if the weight of silence means that this is something the black is consenting to do. This is an expression of language, but that of silence, imposed at best. "Oppressive language does more than represent violence it limits knowledge" (Morrison 2019: 104). This is a form of fabrication, the "*faux*-language" as Morrison states, which creates the climate of silence. This silence is fabricated to be the authorized speech (muted one at that). In fact, the aim of *faux*-language is the incarceration of black speech and cowing it down to silence in order to legitimate the imperial episteme and render it immune from any challenge.

According to the dictates of the imperial episteme, there should be the suspension of being black and, according to this conception, knowledge has nothing to do with human difference. Buying into this hubris of "we are all human" it is as if there are no identities, and this is the way they have been fabricated to suit the violation of the black. It is only if there is a critique of this violation that the black is disciplined and called to transcend race. This is done to distract that black in order not to disturb the continued injustices that are done in the name of language. The black is told to abandon the truth and to follow the illusion of "let us forget about race and move on to build a future." This is done deliberately in order to create a false sense of reality, where the continued impact of racialization should be ignored. This arrogant stance makes the imperial episteme dictate to the black about how to engage epistemic violence and also commands the black to do things without a sense of reflection. Of course, it is absurd to expect what has rendered the black invisible in knowledge to be considerate in any form or have anything to do with the interests of the black. But the point is that the black is engaging in knowledge through whatever means necessary and without seeking any form of permission from the imperial episteme. The black appears on its own in having to engage in the articulation of ideas whose expression must deal with creating the knowledge that is meaningful and compatible with the living world.

The Africanistic presence as an inscription – utterance as it were/embodying full speech – has had to face and contend not only with being estranged and stripped off from any resemblance of familiarity, but radically exteriorized and unimaginable, where even dreaming is turned into a night-marish experience (trauma even; due to the exaggerated negrophobia [racist fantasies as source not symptom] as the legitimated structure of feeling). The absence of the black is what makes the world coherent. Morrison (2019: 144) writes: "The fabrication of the Africanist persona was reflexive; it was an extraordinary meditation of the self, a powerful exploration of the fears and desires that reside in the writerly consciousness (as well as in others), an astonishing revelation of longing, of terror, of perplexity, of shame, of magna-nimity." The *writing off*, as the structured and paradigmatic motif, was well founded and adjusted to make the violation of the black justified as common sense. The erasure of the black is, then, done with ease, with nothing to account for and as if nothing has been or is done to the black. Everything is done to the black and everything is against the black. Everything is done just the way that *it can* be done. There are no consequences as there is no wrongdoing, nothing wrong can be done to the black. As always, the black is always wrong. The black is subjected to dehumanization and what is done is always a "choked representation of an Africanist presence" (Morrison 2019: 114).

On Fabrication

The fabrication of the Africanistic presence is what Morrison shows to be the object, which, under the wanton racial terror, has been one of the primary ways that envision the problematic of race setting in as the institution of reality as such (a fabricated reality so to speak) that, as the institution of markers and symbols, seeks utterance, while the black is muted. This is a way of utterance gagging that is so amorphous, muzzling excess, tongue slicing, and chopping, if not killability, for the being to turn corpse, which can no longer say anything, anymore – dead, dead, dead ... silence! But still, due to the spectral work, there is sayability in what Cervenak (2006: 119) states is "a painful radical semi-incoherence," which marks the language of Morrison's spectral work. Morrison (2019: 141) shows how the ironic Africanistic presence is subjected to distortions and what is revealed is "significant and underscored omissions, startling contradictions, heavily nuanced conflicts," and the problem of dealing with "th[ese] unsettled and unsettling populations." Dealing with the construct of the Africanistic presence and with the problem of race as the center, evasion has been the banality of reality.

> The fabrication of an Africanist persona is reflexive; an extraordinary meditation on the self; a powerful exploration of the fears and desires that reside in the writerly conscious. It is an astonishing revelation of longing, of terror, of perplexity, of shame, of magnanimity. It requires hard work *not* to see this. (Morrison 1992: 12 [emphasis original])

Pressing on:

> Evasion has fostered another, substitute language in which
> the issues are encoded and made unavailable for open debate.
> The situation is aggravated by the anxiety that breaks into
> the discourse of race. It is further complicated by the fact
> that ignoring race is understood to be a graceful, liberal, even
> generous habit. To notice is to recognize an already discarded
> difference; to maintain its visibility through silence is to allow the
> black body a shadowless participation in the dominant cultural
> body. (Morrison 2019: 142)

The ontological absence of the black is legitimated through
and through. Morrison (2019: 142) attests: "The result
has been constant, if erratic, effort to legislate preventative
regulations. There have also been powerful and persuasive
attempts to analyze the origin of racialism itself, contesting
the assumption that it is an inevitable and permanent part
of all social landscape." This has been, in large, the part of
the liberal discourse whose structural act of maintaining the
discourse of the Africanistic presence is to hold and to be held
as the absolute fact. This is something that Morrison (2019:
143) clearly exposes as the imposition of "the 'normal,'
unracialized, illusionary white world that provides the
backdrop for the work." This work of normalizing the black
ontological facticity is real. What is the important task,
which is something clearly evident, is what Morrison (1992:
9) sums as follows: "One likely reason for the poverty of
critical material on this large and compelling subject is that,
in matters of race, silence and evasion have historically ruled
literary discourse." The avoidance of race in its canonical
texts is a lot. What is worth mentioning is the black writerly
voice. Race only comes through when epistemic violence is
pointed out and it would be defended as if knowledge were
immune from racism (or, being racist) – a holy grail and no
criticism should be faced in its direction in order to subject
it to criticism, as this can be taken to be sacrilege of sorts.
Morrison argues clearly that race denialism has been the very
act of exposing racism through the means of criminalizing it;
but this does not change things. In fact, liberal efforts, which

do more work in disguising racism than exposing it, do abate it. What prevails and pervades is the denial of racism. Here is Morrison (1992: 12): "When matters of race are located and called attention to in American literature, critical response has tended to be on the order of a humanistic nostrum – or a dismissal mandated by the label 'political.' Excising the political from the life of the mind is a sacrifice that has proven costly." Race denialism, and its being costly, is as such because of its lobotomizing effect. The avoidance of race as something that is inherent in the imperial episteme (due to its obsession with racism and all forms of dehumanization, where race is the marker) is always what should be put away. Here is Morrison (2019: 164) in amplification: "It always seemed to me that people who wanted the hierarchy of 'race' when it was convenient for them ought not to be the ones to explain it away, now that it does not suit their purpose for it to exist." No amount of race denialism can cover the ontological scandal of dehumanization.

Racialization, a way that race is technologized as an ongoingly permanent organizing principle, meant the imposition of the meaning of color as the marker, which Morrison (1992: 49) articulates as the fact that "this color 'meant' something." The designation of color as the marker is the point of focus and it is the color that is mobilized as something literally common among whites as the marker of difference, and it is projected to those who are dehumanized by the marked, through colorization. Knowledge, in its colonial intention, has been organized to this end and thus been authorized as reality. According to this episteme, color has always meant being degraded from the human status. It is color that has rendered a decree, a call – let there be black killability. Blacks are killed because they have been marked as black.

According to Morrison (1992: 63), "racism is as healthy as it was during the Enlightenment." By its insistence and persistence, it is still there, here and wherever the Africanistic presence is – that is, the iron curtain of antiblackness. Even though it assumes a discursive erasure or embodies a "disguising force" as Morrison states, it is still there as the definer of reality and construction of the world. The ideological agenda has been that of racism in that the configuration of the world has continued to be defined within the constricts of antiblackness.

The fabrication that comes with the colonial apparatus is the one that seeks to create reality and it is as if there is nothing that can be done about it because it is what it is. This is the reality that is made to be unbearable to the black, who are at its receiving end. Their way of life is clutched dehumanization. By legitimating itself, this fabrication is the one of colonization. One of the ways in which fabrication, in a discursive code, the whole symbolic inscription and its internalization, comes through what V. Y. Mudimbe (1988) denotes as "missionary speech," which claims not only to be authoritative, but the sole truth. Its source is claimed to be the divine one. Those who are colonized are made to be the recipients of this speech. The reception means having to inflict colonial wounds, scars, and all maladies of the mind, body, and soul. This vertical speech, this top-down speech, this imposed speech, is a command engineered through violence. It is not only a linguistic current, but it is what necessitates dehumanization. What is said is what is done in the name of dehumanization. That is why the violent mechanics and mechanisms of this speech get justified, or even lubricated to be pious – missionary speech that is. It is the sacred speech, so it claims and anoints itself to be. It justifies itself as not only being for common good, but as the common good in/for itself. In brief, it is the speech of conversion and civilization. It is there to ward off barbarism. This is the embodiment of the missionary speech, which, in attitude, is colonially racist – that is, what Nelson Maldonado-Torres (2007) calls the "imperial attitude." It is this attitude that incubates and proliferates dehumanization by casting the black as barbarian, that thing that contaminates civilization, the thing to be conquered so that it is civilized, but which will never become human. Maldonado-Torres (2007: 245) writes: "The barbarian was a racialized self, and what characterized this racialization was a radical questioning or permanent suspicion regarding the humanity of the self in question."

This speech enables license and, as Ndlovu-Gatsheni (2012) states, the suspension of ethics is there to unleash the manifestation of violence. What this speech concealed is that barbarity of human destruction with which it was paralleled with. It cannot be missed that it is "missionary speech" that is the abettor and justificatory force of what Sabelo Ndlovu-Gatsheni clearly exposes below:

> Hence imperial wars against Indians, Africans, and others were frequently brutal. Genocide, earthed-scotch policies, mutilations of bodies and rape were a legitimate part of "pacification of barbarous tribes." Severed heads of African kinds and chiefs were taken to Europe as trophies. (Ndlovu-Gatsheni 2012: 426)

Those who resist by contradicting it are guilty of profanity. "One might consider that missionary speech is always predetermined, preregulated, let us say *colonized*" (Mudimbe 1988: 47). To amplify Mudimbe, Jean Comaroff and John Comaroff have this to say:

> From the perspective of the missionaries themselves, the effort has two discreet dimensions. The one, aimed at securing converts, was dominated by the sacred narrative, the "good news" of the gospel. The other was the civilizing quest, which involved a struggle over the very fabric and the fabrication, of everyday life. While the first centered most explicitly on the Word and the second on practice, both entailed a mix of utterance and action. Moreover, while separated in evangelical rhetoric, they were mutually entailed aspects of a single initiative; an initiative that turned on a particular kind of pragmatism. (Comaroff and Comaroff 1997: 63)

The embodiment of the missionary speech is colonization. It is a commandment. The missionary speech sees itself as the origin. It is the only speech, the root of invention itself, what Giorgio Agamben (2017: 52) calls a command – "the one who commands is also the first, just as at the origin there is a command." This is the command that must unfold as it is not only at the beginning, but it will inform the whole cause of life and its mutations. At every stage, the command will be there. Since the claim of truth will be established (fabricated as it is), there is a code through which it stands, and colonization is made to be intact in the name of truth. More perplexing is the hypocrisy of dehumanization that is perpetuated in the name of this truth. Undeniably, fabrication is the order of discourse, and life in totality – say, the fabricated reality being installed and imposed under the command. This command comes from the missionary speech. Fabrication, therefore, is made apparent in the dissemination of this speech, whose source is claimed to be the word of God.

> Missionary orthodox speech, even when imaginative or fanciful, evolved within the framework of what, from now on, I shall call the authority of one truth. This is God's desire for the conversion of the world in terms of cultural and socio-political regeneration, economic progress and spiritual salvation. This means, at least, that the missionary does not enter into dialogue with pagans and "savages" but must impose the law of God that he incarnates. All of the non-Christian cultures have to undergo a process of reduction to, or – in missionary language – of regeneration in, the norms that the missionary represents. This undertaking is perfectly logical: a person whose idea and mission come from and are sustained by God is rightly entitled to the use of all possible means, even violence, to achieve his objectives. Consequently, "African conversion," rather than being a positive outcome of a dialogue – unthinkable *per se* – came to be the sole position that the African could take in order to survive as a human being. (Mudimbe 1988: 47–48)

This is fabrication in its highest form as this turned out to be different. Not that it would have been expected that they be otherwise, anyway, because there is nothing truthful in colonization. The missionary speech is a pathological lie. That is why this speech is guised in a form of command. It does not open a room for dialogue because it wants to enforce enclosure. If dialogue is openness – which *it is* – missionary speech is an enforced closure. The command is the first and the last word. Agamben (2017: 52) states that "the origin is always already the command; the beginning is always also the principle that governs and commands."

There is colonization, which fashions itself in a form of what governs and commands. The closed nature of this system is to ensure that it mobilizes violence to justify both its ends and means. It is the imposition that makes itself felt, its presence felt when negating the Africanistic presence, the latter which is systematically and brutally absented.

Since the command has the moral and juridical power, as Agamben notes, colonization makes it easier to make it as the authorized speech, the only speech whose variation of "missionary speech" conceals the dehumanization in the name of salvation; obedience is made to be a matter of truth, the only truth. The Africanistic presence, upon which Morrison (1992) radically insists, presents a scandal to the missionary speech, whose command is nothing but the justification of dehumanization. Mudimbe is also critical of the missionary speech, which propagates itself as the word of God, whereas it was the pathological lie rooted from the colonial tongue. Mudimbe (1988: 52) is calling attention to the modes of "violence in missionary language." By way of a command, the missionary speech, enclosed and enforcing a monologue, demanded obedience from the colonized. In effect, the power of this speech lies in its colonial imperative – the *only word*. It is the word of the world that came into being through a command – that is, the missionary speech as that word of invention.

The fabrication that Mudimbe unmasks is the one that imposes order as the one of Western civilization and Christianity. The submission to the colonial organization of power is what Morrison is resisting.

> The flight from the Old World to the New World is generally seen to be a flight from oppression and limitations to freedom and possibility. Although, in fact, the escape was sometimes an escape from license – from a society perceived to be unacceptably permissive, ungodly, and undisciplined – for those fleeing for reasons other than religious ones, constraint and limitation impelled the journey. All the Old World offered these immigrants was poverty, prison, social ostracism, and, not infrequently, death. (Morrison 1992: 32)

By way of fabrication, is colonization not the imposition of the so-called "Old World" to the colonized? Is it not imposing on the colonized what was escaped from? There is a fabrication that presents a scandal. Derek Walcott says:

> The common experience of the New World, even for its patrician rights whose veneration of the Old is read as the idolatry of the mestizo, is colonialism. They, too, are victims of tradition, but they remind us of our debt to the great dead, that those who break a tradition first hold it in awe. They perversely encourage disfavour, but because their sense of the past is of a timeless, yet habitable, moment, the New World owes them more than it does those who wrestle with the past, for their veneration subtilizes an arrogance which is tougher than violent rejection. They know that [in] openly fighting tradition we perpetuate it, that revolutionary literature is filial impulse, and that maturity is the assimilation of the features of every ancestor. (Walcott 1998: 36)

The New World is the Old World. Even the concept of history is not glory, history is the invention, a fabrication.

> In the New World servitude to the muse of history has produced a literature of recrimination and despair, a literature of revenge written by the descendants of slaves or a literature of remorse written by the masters. Because this literature serves historical truth, it yellows into polemic or evaporates in pathos. The truly tough aesthetic of the New World neither explains nor forgives history. It refuses to recognize it as a creative or culpable force. (Walcott 1998: 37)

Walcott is onto something to hold history to account, to present it as a scandal; or better, to scandalize it. It is one of horror and it continues to endure in the present. The New World, with its claim to be a break, is still scandalized by this history. Walcott (1998: 39) retorts: "The pulse of New World history is the racing pulse beat of fear, the tiring cycles of stupidity and greed." Morrison (1992: 34) writes: "In the New World there was the vision of a limitless future, made more gleaming by the constraint, dissatisfaction, and turmoil left behind." But was there no invention of those who are colonized, and they will be subjected to dehumanization?

What is the scandal then? The Old World was imposed on the colonized. The New World is a fabricated invention. Walter Mignolo (2008) points at how deep is this fabrication, and the blacks were a *tabula rasa* in that they have no state of *a priori* being and are thus rendered absent in the global historical and contemporary picture of time. Morrison (1992: 35) accentuates: "For a people who made much of their 'newness' – their potential, freedom, and innocence – it is striking how dour, how troubled, how frightened and haunted our early and founding literature truly is." Here is a revelation of what has not been a secret:

> Then came the question of enslaved Africans in the New World. Early in the sixteenth century, Indians were considered vassals of the king and serfs of God. Consequently they couldn't be enslaved. This prohibition legitimized the massive enslavement of Africans. (Mignolo 2008: 1737)

Race is always a haunting presence – a reality, the real thing. Morrison (1997: 3) rightfully writes: "I have never lived, nor have any of us, in a world in which race did not matter. Such a world, one free of racial hierarchy, is usually imagined or described as dreamscape – Edeneque, utopian, so remote are the possibilities of its achievement." The haunting permanence of racism means that it cannot be wished away. To do so is just wishful thinking in that reality is denied for what it is and to be evasive about it does not help matters at all. As a matter of fact, the permanence of racism is even haunting Morrison's work. Surely, by Morrison (2019: 159), it is said: "The ideological dependence of racialism is intact." The everyday life of blackness, defined in racial terms, heavily loaded with dehumanizing violence, brought resistance and that as the radical attitude that animates the Africanistic presence. "Encoded or implicit, indirect or overt, the linguistic responses to an Africanistic presence complicate the text, sometimes contradicting them entirely" (Morrison 2019: 160).

The house, the master's house, is what echoes the voice of the master – the White Father – where imperial being is predicated on racism. In the master's house, racism reigns and the laws of the land are the regime of that racism. Therefore, racism is an inescapable fact. By way of writerly combat, writes Morrison (1997: 4): "Counter-racism was never an option." Even this would be a wish, it would remain as such in that it cannot be reality, as blacks do not have the power that comes with institutions nor the symbols that animate reality as such to be racist. The master's house is the antiblack world, and it is racist. The place of dwelling for the black has been non-existent. What Morrison calls home has been a place that the black could not lay claim to. Being homeless and being the pathological object have made homelessness into an audit to which the black is subjected, due to being in the master's house, whose many rooms are haunted by racism, which turns the bodily presence of the black to a mere silhouette in a white wall. The rigid orthodoxies that are imposed on the black do mean being barred from being welcomed in a home. The master's house cannot be reconstructed, decorated, spring-cleaned to be a non-racist house. The racialized body in this house will do nothing. Morrison (1997: 4) is correct: "It is difficult to sign race while designing racelessness." Race is the logic of antiblackness, which has meant the expulsion of the black from humanity. What about having a home in a place that the black is not welcomed – the world? The face of the world and its physiology is racism. That is why the world is antiblack. The house is built in a world, the antiblack world that does not want blacks. The black can be evicted, or the house can be burnt down/demolished at any time should the black claim to be the owner.

According to Morrison, race identification, or it as a point of departure, is insisted upon by the black to show that there is a point of view to be asserted. That, of course, being linked with the lived experience of the black in an antiblack world. This point of view of the black is structurally denied. The point of view of the black is not asserted as a way of generating a discursive engagement. There is no expectation from the black that there will be a moralistic discourse that their oppressors will take into account and have the change of heart that will make them accept the black as the equal. As a way of assertion, the black, according to Morrison (2019: 35), "point of view should not be buried underneath mainstream views and be taken for granted." But still, it is not up to the black to be set the task of making whites treat them in a desired way. The black condition is not what things are and the way they should be. This is still imprinted in the continued existential struggle in which the black continues to engage, as things are supposed to be different. Yes, in forging ahead with this struggle, the desired outcome does not materialize and at most times there are betrayals, disappointments, and defeats. But still, there is a charging continuity. This is the penetration into what has been considered closed, and claimed to be a space – but not for the black.

> In addition, certain absences are so stressed, so ornate, so planned, they call attention to themselves, arrest us with intentionality and purpose, like neighborhoods that are defined by the population held away from them. Looking at the scope of American literature, I can't help thinking that the question should not have been "Why am I, an African American, absent from it?" It is not a particularly interesting query anyway. The spectacularly interesting question is "What intellectual feats had to be performed by the author or his critic to erase me from a society seething with my presence, and what effect has that performance had on the work?" What are the strategies of escape from knowledge? Of willful oblivion? (Morrison 2019: 173)

Morrison problematizes this absence in the light of having made that racism is structural and the prevailing imperial episteme is white. The presence is not begged for by Morrison, but at the heart of her concern is epistemic violence. Morrison (2019: 181) counsels: "A work does not get better because it is responsive to another culture, nor does it become automatically flawed because of that responsiveness." What is at issue is how does the work, the ethos of its episteme and commitment practice, engage the existential questions it comes to face – as the struggle is the existential one – a matter of life and death even? It is the struggle that attests to the fact that the black faces modalities of violence that are surrounding by nature, and whose homicidal mechanics have no regard for the humanity of the black. The epistemic tools that the black put in place through the Africanistic presences are not only the exercises of urgency, but the affirmative politics of self-definition. What should be put in place and should be a way of inhabiting the world, the episteme, as Morrison (2019: 189) states, "requires new kinds of intelligences to define oneself."

On Self-Definition

Self-definition is evident in the ethos of Morrison's Africanistic presence. That is why what comes out is the figure that, in the reconfiguration of the episteme, haunts racist imagination and fantasy. It also poses questions of existence, which have to do with calling to being the insurrection of politics. It is when politics are at the center, where the call for the changing of the *socius* makes sense. The life of the black is the constitutive part of politics. These politics, in their unique character, are politics of existence. They are unique in the sense that existence is affirmed even when it is denied. Therefore, the episteme of the Africanistic presence is both dialogic and dialectic. Both show tensions, exchange, and extension. There are no set outcomes. Unpredictability and uncertainty loom large. The Africanistic presence in its spectral nature means construction and destruction, both in line with the aforementioned dialogic and dialectic language uttered and written with radical expression. There are "counter-discursive narratives," which, as Michelle Wright (2004: 227) puts it, shows the abyss of the black is where "other voices are yet to be heard from." The dialogue and dialectics of the Africanistic presence are blackened by the whole racist machinery. Wright (2004: 71) writes: "White racism, characterized here as spitting, cursing, and the denial of entry, is deemed antidialectical (and therefore antiprogressive) because it attempts to block this move toward synthesis." This structure of onto-epistemological exclusion is deliberate. It is solidified and authorized to keep things as they are and to keep the black out – that is, putting the black in his/her place – placelessness.

At the level of the episteme, it is worth considering what Mudimbe (1993) refers to as the "colonial library." This library invents and constructs the dehumanized figure of the African, the erasure of the Africanistic presence *par excellence*. It is in the colonial library that the black does not have the canonical standing, as well as that thing that constitutes the deficit and lack of being. The colonial library, in its epistemic constitution, makes reference to what is Africanistic presence as *passé*. It is that which cannot be referred to in present terms, or, if it is past, is not worthy of any authoritative status – that is, there is nothing out there. Africa, in the colonial library, "became an indispensable term, a negative trope," as Comaroff and Comaroff (1991: 86) state, the very thing that will be made to be absolute truth – a fabrication indeed. The colonial library houses nothing that is African. The latter is just a silhouette. It is that which is in the dark. The works that are housed in the colonial library are the stereotypical inscriptions whose canonical status is nothing but the static philosophical anthropologies but which are then defended as modern, and nothing archaic is seen about them – for they are episteme *qua* episteme. Their lack of scientific rigor, and absence of the truth they propagated, have been nothing but the knowledge systems that accompany and abate colonialism.

> The symbolic terrain of a rarely seen Africa, then, was being shaped by a cascade of narratives that strung together motley "scientific facts" and poetic images – facts and images surveyed by an ever-more roving European eye. As this suggests, the rhetoric of light and dark, of color and culture, was already palpable in contemporary Europe, though it had not yet taken on the full fan of connotations it was to bear in Victorian thought. (Comaroff and Comaroff 1991: 87–88)

Mudimbe is clear when he points out that the colonial library houses the systems of knowledge that are plagued by "negative metaphors," which painted the negative image of Africa. What the colonial encounter kick-started is dehumanization rationalized as knowledge systems. Mudimbe (1993: 191) contends: "At issue is the experience of history for someone who is excluded from the very archives of history."

With indomitable will to inaugurate another episteme, to erupt from capture, Walcott (1998: 33) delivers weighty questions: "What to do then? Where to turn? How to be true? If one went in search of the African experience, carrying the luggage of a few phrases and a crude map, where would it end?" Being conflicted with searching for purity, and disavowing it to embrace creolization, the different cause of the Africanistic presence is not the search and going back to the origin. Perhaps if these questions could have been directed to the political cause of charting the modes of struggle that disenchant colonization, their mode of address would have been different. Ndlovu-Gatsheni delivers a wise counsel:

> But the most simplistic approach that needs to be avoided at all costs is to consider Africans as a mere datum or census rather than as a collectivity organized in pursuit of a common political and cultural end due to existing diversities. Such a positivist-empirical approach tends to gloss over the fact that the complex question of identity-making itself is a political process mediated through and through by imperatives of inclusion and exclusion. Since the time of colonial encounters Africans have ceaselessly engaged in various political projects within which they continued to struggle to define themselves in political and cultural terms. The best way to approach the idea of Africa and African identities is as political projects mediated by identifiable but complex historical and political process. (Ndlovu-Gatsheni 2013a: 102)

For there must be a chant that disenchants the modern/colonial whose episteme is a dehumanizing force. Ndlovu-Gatsheni (2013a: 100) rightfully writes: "The discursive construction of the 'African people' is a continuing process." It is the construction that runs parallel – the definition of dehumanization that is external and the definition of rehumanization that is internal. It is the continuity of this discursive construction that makes the Africanistic presence to be understood as "the complex state of being and becoming mediated through and through by spatial, agential, structural, historical and contingent variables" (Ndlovu-Gatsheni 2013a: 100). Comaroff and Comaroff (1991: 87) write: "These discourses arose out of a number of distinct but related fields of exploration." The idea and invention of Africa that come from the colonial library are the discursive formation that can be said to be fabrication. Here is Ndlovu-Gatsheni (2013b: 119): "Inevitably Africa is a continent that is ceaselessly seeking to free itself from the Eurocentric egoisms of singularities that continue to inform conventional and often insensitive notions of identities imposed on it and its people by external agents." So, what becomes the discursive formation that informs the epistemology and ontology of the Africanistic presence is what Ndlovu-Gatsheni takes as the combat against "complex externally generated discourses," whose forces of erasure are there to lubricate and solidify colonization. Combat against this dehumanizing force has been that of self-definition. This has been a political project with a long history. Ndlovu-Gatsheni points out clearly that the quest for self-definition is continuous and most enduring in that self-definition has not been an easy project. This was, in fact, "a very complicated socio-political phenomenon" (Ndlovu-Gatsheni 2013b: 124). There are various discourses that inform the Africanistic presence.

> These various discourses of being African leave us with the message that African identity is complex, multi-layered and open to different interpretations. Both the idea of Africa and African identities were and are best understood as states of being and becoming that should be better studied as open-ended and as work-in-progress. (Ndlovu-Gatsheni 2013b: 129)

The genealogies of the Africanistic presence are numerous. One thing that binds them together is the existential struggle to become being and to resist all forces of dehumanization. This is an effort of struggle, of self-definition. Africanistic presence is the struggle of the dehumanized. The nature of this struggle is the refusal to be subjected to the dictates of the colonial library. Ndlovu-Gatsheni (2009: 163) amplifies:

"The struggles of the dominated were ideological, for they necessarily involved an effort to control the cultural terms in which the world was ordered and power legitimated."

The Africanistic presence denotes, epistemologically *stictu sensu*, the figure of the political. The political, according to Anne Garréta (2005), has been the spectral signature of Morrison, and the very duty she duly undertakes. "The return of the political takes the form of a haunting, threatening a collapse of all those painfully (rather than playfully) erected categorical boundaries" (Garréta 2005: 729). This constitution of being is always there, even if such a being is stripped of humanity. By being guided by the act of restoring such a conception, Garréta takes the political as the following:

> The political is not therefore another of the autonomous provinces of culture parceled out by liberalism: it stands outside, beneath, and above. Even more radically, it can be described as *ubiquitous*. Being a pure potential of opposition without a domain or a matter of its own, it can spring up everywhere. It is ever present – if not in actuality, at least in potentiality. (Garréta 2005: 725)

Such is the Africanistic presence that makes Morrison's spectral work, and the oppositional sphere of the political forever reigns as the force of emergence because being forever oppressed will yield rupture. Garréta's skepticism of liberal aspirations, where she insists that they often do not recognize the political in its radical sense, has to do with the ways in which the political has been excluded within the domain of knowledge in favor of a present that points to some abstract nothing, which can even be the antithesis of the political – depoliticized political. According to Garréta (2005: 728), there is "exclusion and waving off of the political ..." This is the problematic of what can, in parallel, be associated with the imperial episteme, which wants nothing to do with the existential predicaments that have to do with the Africanistic presence.

The site where the black originates and dwells is the one of communities in existential struggle. In a collective form, the

Africanistic presence is the place of "epistemic communities," as Corey Walker (2011) states, and it is in these communities that there are dialects, dialogues, and dialectics of struggle whose irresolvable tension does not bring things to a halt but engenders enduring reconfigurations. Walker iterates her argument as follows:

> By recourse to an epistemological investigation and interrogation of local knowledge, we can begin to read more critically and carefully how situated communities construct, mobilize, and deploy knowledge systems that navigate and negotiate the terrain. The conceptualization does not pre-empt the understanding that "knowledge, in particular knowledge of and about the social, is produced in a vacuum." (Walker 2011: 112)

The lived reality of the Africanistic presence has been, all the time, Walker (2011: 114) asserts, about "epistemological positions that develop new epistemic horizons." The configurations with the limits imposed by the imperial episteme do not stand as monuments, shrines, and cathedrals to be worshipped. The ethical attitude that arises to bring into being what has been buried under the structures and to bring insurrection is the very ethos of spectral work, which Morrison engages throughout her corpus.

The terms that are set as hegemonic are now subjected to interrogation, which, then, interrupts what has been static as commonsense. This operation of irruption creates other forms of unfolding, which have been things of the underneath coming to be part of reality on the surface. What has been buried has made a spectral return and thus assumes that the Africanistic presence will ward off the liberal consensus and the racist status quo. Instituting the modes of the episteme, the assertions on which the black embarks, is the way to (re)formulate critique. The protocols of the episteme have to do with voicing the narrative that could not be heard. The contradicting position to which the black has been relegated is a species of the isolated, the position of the outside, exteriority *par excellence*. The expulsion from humanity has put the black into a position where it is said to have brought nothing to the field of knowledge. However, this is deemed flawed and false – the falsehood of triumph guised as altruism. Even those well-evidenced and justified submissions that are made by the black to the world will still be subjected to doubt and utter denial. The denial of black humanity is what Morrison grapples with and to challenge the abject conditions that the black is in are ruins from where knowledge originates. This, as a way of remaking the world, is also a way of making it. By refusing to succumb to the sensitivities that claim knowledge to be neutral and far from the enterprise of dehumanization, it is at the heart of the Africanistic presence that discursive practices refuse to be turned into apologia. The combat of truth-telling is necessary to cause the mask that conceals barbarity in the name of civilization to come off and fall.

> If we follow through on the self-reflexive nature of these encounters with Africanism, it falls clear: images of blackness can be evil *and* protective, rebellious *and* forgiving, fearful *and* desirable – all of the self-contradicting features of the self. Whiteness, alone, is mute, meaningless, unfathomable, pointless, frozen, veiled, curtained, dreaded, senseless, implacable. (Morrison 1992: 59)

Morrison comes to this conclusion, as a cartographer of existence and as having surveyed the literary landscape of white writing, which pathologizes blackness and valorizes whiteness. The fact of whiteness as impenetrable and its being a ward-off for the black, is a discursive closure. It has the double drift of elevating itself, while downgrading the black to the point of absolute elimination, and this qualifies Morrison's conclusion. If the ontology of the black does not exist, then there is no narrative of the ontology of blackness. Also, then, there is no ontology of that narrative. Nothing was said. No one said anything. There is nothing to such an extent that there is no episteme. When the black is forcibly introduced into the field of knowledge, then, there is a shout that this is a cause for disaster. There is doubt, impasse, stasis. These structured sensibilities, silly ones at that, are combatively engaged through Morrison's spectral work to haunt commonsense and thus to put the liberal consensus under pressure, where its center cannot hold to form an embodied totality. What emerges from Morrison's spectral work is the destruction of the narrative – the nonsense of what makes sense – or, the absence of the very sense even in that common sense and, if this is such a situation, then there is no sense that can be traced. If the black is what is the outside sense or any sense, then, *a priori*, the black is, according to imperial episteme, an anomie that cannot be reconciled with the way things have been, are, and will be. The black cannot be incorporated into anything that has to do with sense. The Africanistic presence that Morrison authorizes has been a subject of interrogation, with the end result of its being dehumanized. Morrison (1997: 10) writes: "It is more urgent than ever to develop an epistemology that is neither intellectually shunning nor self-serving reification." When the black takes the Africanistic presence as the locus and point of departure (without any quest for redemption, resolve, or restoration) there lies a start to begin the narrative, that first utterance whose stuttering is bearing in mind that the battle has begun and Africanistic presence from the perspective of black authorization is denied. The knowledge validity of the black will always be subject to doubt and that means the black is not there.

Writing the horror of the everyday life and the spectral work being the agenda of Morrison, Ronald Judy (1993) argues that this form of writing is thanatology, in that it is a writing that is located in the taxonomy of death and reason. Writing as the work of death is, according to Judy, "horrible labor." It is coming into contact and being entangled with horror. By writing this horror, bringing it to the world, Morrison's episteme is horrible labor. It is the labor that is attuned to the working of death to which the black has been structurally and systematically subjected. The thanato-political nature of this also lends itself to facing death, being inscribed by it and subjected to its name. Death as the end is the inscription of the signature that closes a file – case closed! Death is the end. Nothing comes after death. But Morrison rewrites death by mobilizing spectrality and makes the everyday thing of the living. The stir that Morrison makes generates the episteme that militates against the finality that is imposed by the imperial episteme, which relegates the black to absolute absence, to hyper-invisibility. Judy lays a reminder:

> It is not to be forgotten that the abject muteness of the body is not to exist, to be without effect. Writing the death of the African body is an enforced abstraction. It is an interdiction of the African, a censorship to be inarticulate, to not compel, to have no capacity to move, to be without effect, without thought. (Judy 1993: 89)

The rewriting of the episteme by Morrison in forging ahead registers that blurred finality, whose unethical judgments against the black have been done on grounds that have nothing to do with any form of discursive engagement by the commandment of what Judy calls "interdiction." The enforced abstraction that Judy highlights is key to understanding how the black has been emptied of all the ontological content of being, and has been rendered a thing that can be subjected to all forms of epistemic violence without any accounting. The writing that is called for by Morrison, the one of reconfiguring the episteme through rewriting, is deemed a threat to the status quo and should be interdicted at all times because it is "disturbing the peace." Nothing should be said. The reign and weight of muteness should prevail. The condition of writing under erasure becomes an imposed structure of enforced abstraction; the writing of the black is the deliberate act of making the black not to feature anywhere in the field of knowledge. Morrison insists on rewriting, and it should be so. In amplification, Judy (1993: 87) writes: "The work of writing is to offer relief though resurrection of the demise [of] body as a representative trace."

On Spectral Writing

From Morrison's spectral work, there emanates critique that animates questions, the interrogation of utterances and their reception; and also has to account for ways of closure, if not the killability of the black not to utter anything and to let silence reign. There is no utterance, or, in a form of inscription, what Morrison (1992) calls "literary utterance." For there to be literary utterance or full speech in the sense of having to embody blackness, the Africanistic presence should be its own authorial inscription and its discursive chains of whiteness should be broken completely. This, in all accounts, is self-construction, which should not be maligned, but aligned. The cultivation of consciousness (which is not a one-off event but comes to reality in order to wake up from slumber [rude-awakening so to say] and is the build-up from strength to strength) creates the vision in which the envisioned self should be the one that sees things for what they are. The Africanistic presence means seeing a nightmare in what is called "The African Dream" and it is the rude awakening that will prevent the illusion from being mistaken for reality. What is thinkable is what the imperial episteme makes available because the spark of imagination is extinguished before a flame could light up. The unthinkable, what is still in the dark, the unseen if not the non-existent, is what opens a way for the Africanistic presence to drill and crack all closures. What the opening ensures, it will not be the doors that are opened for the black. The key has been thrown away. The black has been thrown deep down into the dungeon, the abyss – that is, the imperial episteme declares by way of a decree to the black in the language of the absolute law: "darkness has been cast upon thee." It is the radical opening of the black that comes to challenge this darkness, to render the "mighty speech" of the imperial episteme as not being absolute. What is insisted upon is the radical presence of the black, whose terms are in sync with black aspirations. Here, it is not a matter of what the white wants for humanity, but what the black wants. Whiteness has and will never have any interests for the black.

The ontological denigration of the black means that there is no speech. Nothing can be said, and this is because the speech has been *a priori* claimed absent by whiteness speaking on behalf of the black. What is verbalized, if it were to be listened to, white auditory faculties get to be decoded and encoded as the absence of speech; but something that is absent is said to be language itself.

What will be the narrative of the Africanistic presence in the continued muting presence of the imperial episteme? In what ways will the Africanistic presence articulate another speech? The answer to these interrelated questions is that the Africanistic presence is a speech in its own right. It seeks no audience for what renders it absent. For those who dwell in the Africanistic presence, the speech has been there – laments, cries, screams – terror, terror, terror ... What has been said is *racial terror.* The imperial episteme, with its multiple forms of oppression, does not want to be confronted for the devastating violation it structurally metes out. It does not attend to the ways that it oppresses even in its "innocent knowledge" production, which, in fact, is laced with racialization and its resultant dehumanization. The epistemic defects and deflects of any meaningful knowledge expression have this contradiction, which normalizes a paternalistic pattern, where epistemic violence epidermalizes itself. This speech cannot be overly emphasized. Of course, deafness is what confronts this speech and added to it has been technology of silence. Enclosed whiteness. It does not want to be seen for what it is. The narrative is of the black as gagged, thus unseen.

What the Africanistic presence calls for is something different, an alternative that has not been fed with the desire for relevancy and popularity of the mainstream. In fact, the utterances occur from the muted place. Paul Moya (2011) calls for the disturbing of the status quo and to chart alternative forms of knowledge. In addition, it is also important to highlight this:

> Such alternative perspectives call to account the distorted representation of peoples, ideas, and practices whose subjugation is fundamental to the maintenance of an unjust hierarchical social order. Consequently, if we as scholars are interested in having an adequate – that is, more comprehensive and objective, as opposed to narrowly biased in favor of the status *quo* – understanding of a given social issue, we will listen harder and pay attention to those who bring marginalized views to bear on it. We will do so in order to counterbalance the overweening

> "truth" of the views of those people in positions of dominance whose perspectives are generally accepted as "mainstream" or "common-sense." (Moya 2011: 85)

The production of knowledge from this end means having to confront the imperial episteme with its overbearing truth, which, in the sense of its commonsense, cannot be the totality of reality and the world. The marginalized and excluded locales produce knowledge that bears testimony to the modes of struggle that shape life. The imperial episteme is there to reinforce "structures that buttress the hierarchies of knowledge to which we have all become accustomed" (Moya 2011: 90). The interruption that comes with the Africanistic presence, which shakes the solidity of these structures and disseminates the knowledge that confronts these very same structures, is a facticity that becomes too much to bear. What will happen, predictably so, is the demonizing of epistemic protocols of the Africanistic presence as being questionable and thus not being knowledge at all.

Since the position of where the utterance originates is one of the most important epistemic concerns (which is largely ignored by the imperial episteme and its pretense of neutrality and abstract universalism), this is the protocol that is necessary to engage in a fundamental critique of antiblackness. For the black to be put in this dehumanizing condition, there should be utterances that do not disavow their *loci* and *foci*.

> What I am pointing to here is that those who are most likely to attend to the dynamics of one of the kinds of oppressions are usually those situated on the downside of some corresponding and relatively intractable power relation that serves to structure our global society, while those who do not attend to that oppression are usually those situated on the upside of that power relation. (Moya 2011: 79)

Spectrality also reigns, even without so much power, due to the forces of interdiction and hypocritical commonsense that yield the liberal consensus that the world of the human should be preserved, and the black should stop the victimhood in the act of making the utterance that bears any semblance to the Africanistic presence. This form of censure reigns because it is the colonial/racist order of things and how the *polis* should be protected from tyranny and anarchy. The black is ontologically criminalized and pathologized in order not to have any form of epistemic legibility. Nothing the black says, in the totalizing banality of the liberal consensus, will be taken up or seriously as valid. The validity of the black is subjected to invalidation.

What do we make of the life that has not been valued as life, which has not been permitted to live in the first place? The black is such a conundrum, which underlies and under-lines the necessity of this question. In search of forms of lives, and having been denied life itself, the black is dreaming of a better world, a dream that the black evokes to enact possi-bility (Cervenak 2016). Cervenak (2016: 2) writes: "This is the figure who treats the edge of day, roaming the margins of enlightened society in search of its tossed-aside forms. Forms that once held taxonominable, catalogable, nameable life." Is Cervenak's formulation not bearing accountability to the spectral work that Morrison undertakes? On the affirmative – yes! By engaging in this kind of spectral work, Morrison revitalizes by creating life forms and by wanting the unwanted, remaking what has been destroyed, sentencing what has been split, if not ripped apart. Formations of deformations are what drive Morrison's spectral work; the refusal to die where forms are made to, according to Cervenak (2016: 3), "allow for their weightedness to return;" durability as it were, and the way life is enabled in the face of structured death.

The materiality of life is echoed in the epistemic enter-prise that does not seek to be the exchangeable object, the commodity refused, the value that does not seek validity of the market, but the political value that creates the intramural value of the black. It is the black whose consciousness means Africanistic presence as the knowledge of the self that is bound by itself, not as the object that avails itself of epistemic violence. It is the self that comes to itself by making the episteme to be the cartographic inscription of the *elsewhere*, the place that the black desires.

The violence that the black experiences and endures in everyday life is so unbearable that it has, paradoxically, become banal in that it does not raise any alarm that will make it come to a complete end. The condition of black exclusion and its rampant violence has marked itself as a condition that will remain the same and with no dose of redemption in sight. The violence against the black is one of the haunting things that plague the black bodily life and, if this were to be inscripted to the living to the literal expression, still, there is no language to account for this brutality. Jared Sexton (2015) points out clearly that there is no sanctuary for the black, and there is nowhere the black can turn in order to hold the world accountable. The very dehumanization of the black is the way in which the world makes sense of itself. That is to say, the coherence of the world is contingent upon the absolute destruction of the black. Here is Sexton:

> You live out a valueless form of life whose value exists as potential in and of another world, a higher-dimensional space. You cannot protect yourself and you will not be saved. You will learn that lesson to the young ones and pass it on to them as a mission or a curse. You cannot protect them with your love and advice and no one has yet devised an art of war sufficient to the task. The hatred of the world is upon you. It is also within you. (Sexton 2015: 162)

The existential fight is the one that does not play in the gallery of "I am human too," when the humanity of the black is denied. Plainly, there is no need for the black to prove the worth of its humanity. There is no need for dialogue, as this will prove futile because the statement of dehumanization is final – a monologue. What can become a way of a radical will and testament, as Sexton shows, is not the humanistic gesture of the black. This gesture submits to the crowding out of the liberal consensus. Also, to note, Morrison's gesture, that of the radical will that Sexton hints at, is far from being a tool that can be used by the liberal consensus to take the radical will of blackness.

Let us assume that the concept of the human, or a certain dominant conception of the human, stands in the way of any collectivity and insurgent revaluation of black life as such. Yet the specter of captivity and condition of impossibility for the displacement of the human as such. (Sexton 2015: 163)

Morrison's claims to knowledge are not immune from being appropriated and disfigured. The specter that continues to haunt, but one that is prevented from being a register, finds expression by having to be a mode of a potent radical insistence.

The horror that blackness experiences is the result of repeated ammunition of antiblackness. To declare one to be human and be worthy to embody this episteme is not a central concern here. What is key, fundamentally, is the spectral persona of the black. To be there while rendered spectral is, in a sense, that ghost who is there but also not there – that something in between. But the ghost is there. There is haunting going on. It does not stop. There is some work going on – that spectral writing that bears Morrison's episteme, her signature. This spectral work, one that rewrites the episteme, is not only caught in the correlative sign, it does, by radical intent (and pointedly so) combatively assume the authorial inscription of blackness. Morrison has this to say:

They can serve as allegorical fodder for the contemplation of Eden, expulsion, and the availability of grace. They provide paradox, ambiguity; they reveal omissions, repetitions, polarities, reifications, violence. In other words, they give the text a deeper, richer and more complex life than the sanitized one commonly presented to us. (Morrison 2019: 160)

There is a lot to be unearthed that must be brought to the surface. The body of criticism that comes as a result of the assertion of the Africanistic presence should be frank and telling-it-like-it-is. Morrison (2019: 160) declares: "It would be a pity if the criticism remained too polite or too fearful to notice a disrupting darkness before its eyes."

Those who are not valued are said not to have any epistemic value and this is rooted in the fact that they are dehumanized. The troubling nature of blackness, its haunting status, does not yield possibility to the grounding force of politics. The way the world is, in its antiblack nature, does not want the black to be in the realm of the human.

The problematic of the Africanistic presence is spectrality. It is, by way of Melanie Anderson (2013), the problematic of spectrality that is forever present, where some aspects of Morrison's body of works can be regarded as "haunted texts." The untold story, the narrative absence, which has the sayability, it being said amid censure anyway, can be regarded, in the present, as a form of spectrality. In terms of rewriting knowledge, Morrison is said to be writing, according to Anderson (2013: 2), "spectral work," which is mandated with the commitment "to subvert the master narrative" as the totalizing episteme. The Africanistic presence, as a problematic, is a shadow that refuses to be ignored and the present becomes, because of being pushed to transform (whether this materializes or not). The demand for anything or things to transform, and getting to work for such transformation to begin, continue, or materialize is, in the current order's stasis, the making of things to be different or otherwise. The present cannot be what it used to be. This interruptive moment (the insistence of transformation) makes the living present to be a troubled one in that it is shaken by the transformative force that is embedded in Morrison's spectral work. The scene of writing, the haunted scene, is what haunts the present. The inscriptive antagonism, the mode of literary combat as it were, writing becomes the fiber of existence, the documenting not of the everyday life of the black, but the invention of the life in the way that it should be. Thus, the coherent code is broken by spectrality, where other forms of lives are summoned to appear, and the ways of writing that are inhabited in that cosmos of marginality come to the center. "Morrison's specters bring attention to the veiled spots in history and those horrifying events that defy description, those places where mainstream America does not want to shine a light" (Anderson 2013: 148). This light cannot be dimmed. What shines will be the hallo, ghost-like, which shows that there is something out there in the dark.

In darkness, there lies the episteme – Morrison's spectral work, which names knowledge for what it is and in her own terms. The potency of this register of the episteme, the way of authorizing as it were, the authorship of blackness, is the generativity of bringing what is near and far, ruptured and sutured, strange and familiar into coalescence without the unified end. The invention of the extreme, where contacts are potentialized, brings to the fore the connective sensibility where the system of thought is not clinically reduced to polarities. In ontological terms, the living and the dead are made to be embodied in one.

The problematic of being disjointed is what African presence must confront. Nothing can be cut off in terms of not having epistemic validity because it is named and demonized as such by the Western canonical formation. Things that are said to be of no standards can, from the everyday life of the black, form the important basis from where life and thought generate life words that are worthy of study.

Spectral work is the onto-epistemological presence that is rendered absent. The work itself is subjected to the weight of misrecognition and erasure. It is as if there was or is nothing there. This is done in the infrastructure of denial. The Africanistic presence as the spectral work is conjuring, its invented absence cannot be a source of comfort, but there is what is always spectrally lingering – a different episteme that is out there, which shakes the foundation of the Western lies.

Of Wandering

Africanistic presence is, according to the precise formulation of Cervenak (2015), "wandering," which, by the way, is a way of freedom, of fugitivity. Being unwanted in the world of the human, the black is relegated to the margins of existence: like the ghost spirit that lingers, the black wanderer, the enforced. What becomes evident is the spirit of restlessness, or what Carol Schmudde (1992) calls "restlessness of the spirit," where wandering bears the weight and burden that possess the black.

Wandering bears with it the unseen movement, which can be on the ground or underground. Like the ghosts who haunt, they can be seen or remain unseen. The place of wander, or the place where wandering takes place, is not a fixed place, but where there is the creation of other words. Narratives in which Morrison engages are located in the making and unmaking of the world. These narratives of wandering do not invent in composition but decomposition. Cervenak (2015: 143) accentuates: "Wandering describes the conditions of possibility of their (de)composition, as wandering is enacted by writers and storytellers and readers and listeners."

What lies at the heart of Morrison's episteme is transgression and transcendence of the regulatory force that disciplines the black, and what is couched is the rupture of possibilities of the phenomenon that exceeds, and which creates the condition of what can be graspable. This is the installation of freedom, freedom to move, and to be moved by freedom. Here Cervenak (2015: 144) pushes on to write: "To wander is to renounce the limit imposed on one's movement, to live and act in excess of the moorings of someone else's desire. To make and unmake one's way." If the black ways of thinking, knowing, and doing were permission-seeking exercise, there would be no freedom. Instead, there would be limits, stasis, and decadence. The moves that are inhabited in wandering are acts of freedom, the quest for it, and ceaseless struggle for it in the face of constant disappointment. The way the black says things and thus mobilizes the narratives of freedom is the mode of insisting and instituting the forms of life that are inherently denied. In so doing, they live otherwise; they have their own way of living.

Furthermore, Morrison's refusal to be disciplined, ordered, straightened out, is a radical commitment to wander and to really busk in haunting reality. This is the condition that articulates the narrative of existence. The way of knowing the precarity of black life, its deadliness, is curatorial practice, which pushes for the understanding of the workings of death. To confront death by killing the paralyzing fear that comes from not wanting to be subjected to lethal racist violence, the production of *knowledge otherwise*, the black episteme in

Morrison, gives the radical insistence to live. This insistence is not that of mere life as dictated by fear, but necessary life as dictated by the absence of fear.

Again, Morrison's refusal leads her to assume the position that she is reduced to as the black, as the figure of the outside that cannot be allowed to go loose, to stand in combat and to refuse the dictates of the "straight text," as Cervenak points out, comes as the form of writing that is the disciplining tool. It is the straight text that straightens the black. But the antithesis to this is to wander. The black, by way of Morrison's corpus, wanders by veering off from the straight text. Wandering as a persistent (un)making of knowledge is Morrison's code. The weight of narratives that come to be told are what Cervenak names "unnarrated sojourns," because they are yet to be told and there is no grammatical reception or institutions of code deciphering a place for them. The grammars of existence are so contentious in that the antiblack world refuses to dialogue with them as they present the onto-epistemological scandal, where what is supposed not to speak or have any form of articulation or to embody any form of existence makes incommunicability to be the order of things. The route of *knowledge otherwise*, the radical refusal to be subjected to the straight text, is to engage in a form of writing that sets wandering to be a form of rupture against all sorts of orthodoxies and forms of violence that imprint them.

If things are scriptural, it is clear that Morrison un-scripts them through wandering. The form of writing she embodies and expresses is not the sole entity of a single story, but the script writes the un-scripted to have more and more narratives as troubling things for the Western hegemonic textual closure. The straightening of the black is for the sole purpose of depoliticization and is to further pathologize black existence as not being worthy. Those who take the mantle of doing what is necessary see that the kind of knowledge that is produced refuses to be further disciplined. Knowledge is expressed in its own terms – highly politically charged – a decisive move, wandering. This is against being straightened out, and thus shows the precise point of the terms that stand against being violated. In essence, it is to be subjected to the dialectics of the un-scripted text.

The black episteme that Morrison asserts is, therefore, the move without constraint and restraint. Freedom is not a given. It is made. It is not there. It is a matter of fact, a matter of life, of death even. "Indeed, wandering, in its engagement with actual and phantasmatic terrain, queries the complexity, range, and meaning of freedom as movement" (Cervenak 2015: 147). The liberal illusion that freedom is a given and that it is for all humans, does not attend to the blackened scandal where freedom is known as scarcity or absolute absence. The stakes are high for the black, the fight for freedom is a necessity, which is often violated. To practice freedom, to wander, the black is in a lethal condition. The kind of writing that emerges from Morrison's episteme cannot be delinked from the risk that it is in. There is no option to take but risk. To conquer fear and set the chart to move forward is the freedom to move a lethal affair. It is to do nothing but to keep on moving – to wander. The black is "wandering in the wilderness" as Schmudde (1992: 409) states, and here that is "increasingly intrusive manifestations of haunting until that conflict is resolved by the exorcism of the ghost." The time in which Morrison writes and which is a spectral moment, of course, is an inauguration of, as Christina Sharpe (2016: 13) illuminates, "a kind of blackened knowledge, an unscientific method, that comes from historical and ongoing rupture." The integrum of time, the haunted scene of the antiblack world, is a plane that is subjected to the existential struggle for it to end.

Things are put into question, into perspective. They are what they are supposed to be. For, in the present condition, they are not what they are supposed to be. It means, then, the status quo is haunted. It is, as a scene, a haunted scene. The way of narrating this condition is having to come to terms with Morrison's spectral work, where the haunted scene becomes a place that is subjected to forensic investigation. The scene is that of the antiblack world, and it is where the crimes against the black have been committed without restraint. Those who are subjected to the spectral livelihood are blacks who, according to Sharpe, are refused from being granted life and are those who died in a state of being what she calls "impenitential" because they are unwritten from the scriptural embodiment of the human. The continued terror to which the black is subjected has the capacity to produce life. Or, the black is asked to survive in this terrible condition. The reason for this has been, according to Sharpe (2016: 116), "an ongoing present of subjection and resistance." It is here that haunting imprints itself as the status quo is disturbed. The terrain that adds to a pressure point at times becomes an offshoot of violent rupture and many times has seen black resistance being mercilessly crushed (or even coopted to reproduce the status quo). There are ways of being that radically insist on living even in the face of disappointment or failed revolutions. Sharpe (2016: 22) writes: "If we are lucky, the knowledge of this positioning avails us of particular ways of re/seeing, re/inhabiting, and re/imaging the world. And we might use these ways of being in the wake of our responses to terror and the varied and various ways that our Black lives are lived under occupation." This is evident in Morrison's episteme that the struggle for existence and having to face the weight of antiblackness shows that things have fundamentally to change.

The reconfiguration of the episteme, rewriting from the position of Africanistic presence is, more fundamentally, doing critical work, the work not only of critique, but the affirmative register of refiguring. It is the work of antagonism, where spectral presence means having to remain resolute and radically committed to the persistence of liberation. The renewed writing that comes with the Africanistic presence is not wasted in the idea of the originary and the purist, but the decoding and indexing of what has been structurally fixed allows the set-in robust critique. This is necessary as the life of the black is, according to Neferti Tadiar (2015), subjected to orderly modes of interdictions and annihilation. This, according to Tadiar (2015: 146), is "discursive means of imperialist reproduction." The way of putting a stop to the perpetual marginalization and exclusion of the black in the realm of the episteme has been instituted through coding and indexing.

The spectral nature in which the existential struggle ensues while it is being prohibited is the very thing that makes the insistent violence not to be feared but rather haunted. Even though this violence cannot be stopped by moral acts and its benevolence is the maintenance of the status quo, the radical unmasking of it is the drive for the antiblack world to cease to exist. The acts of haunting are necessary to account for those who passed and who are clouded and chained by fear not to act. The concern for life that is valuable to be lived and, yet, one that is outside the reach and firm grasp of the black, is a project that Morrison's spectral work is forging ahead as the possibility of impossibility. This is the project of instituting life. In the affirmative, Tadiar (2015: 148) writes: "For life-making, perhaps especially under the condition of foreclosure, negation, and dispossession, may very well and often does consist of practices that can corrode rather than preserve the putative sociality of one's naturalized belonging, in part by involvement in and mediations about other socialities." It is worth considering, perhaps, the ways in which spectral work is the very form of life-making. For it is the mediation of life and death, the co-constitution and that as the institution of the work of writing. This does not mean the imperial justification of thanato-politics, but the work of life – life-making. The imperial episteme is confronted head-on, and its foreclosures are outdone by inventions whose potency is holding life, even if it is mere survival. What emerges from Morrison's spectral work is how life is made and how persistent modes of living are instituted by trying to bear capacities of generativity whose creativity means extendability overcoming disposability. Even though disposability reigns, there are insurgent ways that come to claim life and the rewriting of the episteme is the renewal project of "life of communities" as Tadiar affirms, the collective engagement of politics of knowledge that is attuned and attentive to radical possibilities of life-otherwise. The conclusive analytical question Tadiar poses is instructive and very central to the Africanistic presence as articulated by Morrison:

Now do we mobilize other social analytics to bring into operation remaindered forms of social intelligence, imagination, and is given in empire and the very frames within which such things (like "race as difference") are given but also, in doing so, how do we set the stage (create the platforms) for radical departure from the given condition of life under empire now? (Tadiar 2015: 156)

The ghost is not in the memory of the living. The ghost is not obliterated from the memory of the living and ghost occupies the space of the dead and the living (Schmudde 1992). The plunge into the horror of existence is what Morrison's narrative is all about. Spectrality has to do with contained political assertion, authorization of memory work. Saidiya Hartman (2002) shows how the acts of remembering in the living presence are effaced, and this even means that the dead are not safe. Hartman (2002: 758) contends: "Yet how best to remember the dead and represent the past is an issue fraught with difficulty, if not outright contention." Morrison's spectral work is often dismissed on top of its being the episteme of the radicalized life. The onto-epistemic injuries that have been the scarifications of the black are "inflected anew," as Hartman would state, and she questions how, in this continued violence, healing and mourning can take place, where what is mourned is continuing to agonize in the present. Clearly, Morrison's spectral work is informed by the reality of being structured in the state of "irreparability," which Hartman locates as subjection of black bodies – the injury without end. This continuum exists because of "the broken promises of freedom," as Hartman (2002: 760) punctuates. More so, there is no way that this cannot evoke the spectral work that refuses to forget and that also refuses to decenter the dead, who died from the exact violence that marks the present and the banality of the everyday because it is routinized and peppered with a high dose of depoliticization, which calls for amnesia – through political triumphalism and its romanticist decadence. How can there be mourning of terror that continues to be subjected to memory work? This is a different question and one that still haunts because it is spectral in nature.

The reign of silence is the face of epistemic violence, where the black is in the arena of nothingness and where thought and any form of subjectivity are rendered non-existent. There is just nothing there. Therefore, there must be the reign of silence. This becomes a well-maintained status as the inner-workings of epistemic violence institute that silence through the righteousness/absolute truth that will make it impossible for the black utterance to falsify the epistemic statement that it confronts. The black is no one. No one is there. There has never been anyone. The being of the black is the being of no one. This is the no one with no name. Even if the black will pronounce her or his name, this name is still the name of no one. There is nothing; there is nothing out there. That which bears no name is nothing and to extend this, it does not exist. This is the logic of whiteness, anyway. This namelessness, which is something with which the black is attacked, becomes personified to the point of criminalization and pathologization (Morrison 1992). This act of dehumanizing is rendering absence where "narrating and presenting," according to Morrison, the acts of speech, of authorizing one's name to avoid namelessness, will collapse into meaninglessness. Namelessness and meaninglessness are what whiteness entangles in order to abstract the black, to empty all forms of narrating and presenting as mute.

In the face of epistemic violence Morrison insists on the imperative of critical investigation, and this means that the epistemic of the elsewhere, the one that dwells in the pathologized existence, is struggling to dismantle the solidity of the imperial episteme. This means severing from the chains and constraints that would deputize the epistemic rupture that would inaugurate the Africanistic presence. The contention has been the master narrative that has been despotically enthroned as both reality and the world. Not that this is a given. The violent constructions and their perpetuation in a form of colonial structures of knowledge, present and propagate themselves not only as authoritative, but as absolute ends.

Morrison (1992: 53) calls for attention to be paid, at least, to rewriting the episteme, as this will usher in "a much more complex and rewarding body of knowledge." This means having to conduct the necessary critical investigation about the Africanistic presence as the epistemic ground, source, fulcrum, and orbit, where reality of the world is read differently and from vast and contrasting points that are not divorced from the lived embodied experience of the black. Such analyses will reveal, according to Morrison, the rupture of the surface on which blackness dwells on its underground, and for it to be present and to present their own episteme. Everything is taken away from the black, including knowing itself.

Morrison's imperative of rewriting the episteme is not about the outcome. It bears semblance to the labor that confronts horror. Without losing sight of the real, which is linked to the very failure or disappointment, Morrison departs from the rewriting will as if it were the first act of commitment – as if there has not been an existential struggle crushed before. Thinking from this limit, the excavation of potentiality whose will is indomitable, the amount of energy, the power of rewriting, the epistemic is the actual fulfillment of what is the imperative. It is to *start there* and to *hold on there* because that is a site of struggle; because the humanistic struggle is not the one that will make the imperial episteme to accommodate any form of Africanistic presence. The black demand for freedom is ceaseless. This is the inexhaustible nature of writing the black episteme. There lies the knowledge that crafts a solid critique of the imperial episteme, which can no longer claim the sovereign status of being a canon. Morrison's Africanistic presence is the rewriting of the episteme that shakes the surface from its underneath. This is the project of the emergence of life. It is the resurrection of those who are possessed with the indomitable will to live in the terms that are set and dictated by them. Even if their efforts are denied, they insist on life differently – otherwise, anyway, and anyhow.

3

"Sophisticated Lady" –
On Phonographic Authorship

The way of having to think through Hortense J. Spillers demands an examination of how she refigures phonography. This is by means of her radical practice and, as a figure of the black, she writes by way of her freedom practices. By refiguring phonography, Spillers undertakes a different form of writing, whose advocacy for freedom is a relentless pursuit of ending all forms of dehumanization. To proceed, by way of attesting to how Spillers is a sophisticated lady, one who is black, a question needs to be posed in relation to the aforementioned statement that bears the opening line of this meditation. It will be argued, therefore, that this statement is underwritten by a fundamental question, and it is posed thus: In what form, formulation, and formation can musicality be extended as the marker of Spillers's sophisticated writerly practice?

The sophisticated lady is not that doll, a cosmetic thing, an object of desire, but a sophisticated thinker, a radical one at that. Spillers is that sophisticated thinker who can be revered or loathed. This does not make her change her stance to what she deems palatable, she thinks, says, and does what must be done, in ways that charge forth for freedom as it has to be lived. Even if this freedom is not realized, the radical effort of Spillers's work, by the fact of her being black and writing with so much critical passion about matters of black life, she stands on and for the cause. By phonographic writing, this meditation accounts for the ways that the *sound* of blackness is captured and accounted for in Spillers's critical thought.

The fabric of the black life is the canvas on which phonographic authorship is forever apparent and it is a distinct form of writing, which Spillers embodies. It is the writing that results from the radical practice of refiguring itself. It is the birth of the original. Here, sophistication is what is original. More pointedly, it is whatever that is in the name of the original. To add to this, it is a rebirth. What comes from Spillers is everything that has to do with this rebirth. Yes, phonographic authorship is such.

What can be clearly stated is that not only does Spillers write (about) music, but she is the one who, in her vernacularity, spits, splits, and spills it. In this phonographic authorship, form is subjected to extension, expansion, exhaustion. This is the rebirthing whose rethinking comes in the name of refiguring, and Spillers is located as the one who is concerned with the phonographic matter that is pushed to the limits of writing – the *otherwise*.

By statement and standing, the sophistication of Spillers lies in her giving it her all for the life that is lived in the name of freedom, whose radicality stems from everything being at stake in so far as black life is concerned and that demands a note (say, the blue note as the critical assertion and a response even) to testify to the dark times she is in. Even if that freedom is not there, being in relentless pursuit of it is the mark of sophistication. That feeling, and the effect of being touched, are the sophistication of good stuff. This is what is deep and interesting. Spillers, in accounting for the idea of deep stuff, is interfaced with Charles Mingus. What is reconfigured here is how the composition "Sophisticated Lady" is a matter of critical thought. A narrative is not given about the composition, but it is put forth as something of depth, what is worthy to be engaged as a matter of critical thought. It is here where phonographic authorship will be meditated upon in order to reconfigure the critical thought of Spillers.

Of Scripting Sound

So, where is the next place to go when having to think about the refiguring of the phonographic matter, as a matter of an earlier-stated interface, if not to Mingus? His musical testament, his larger-than-life persona, has everything to do with the statement and material of the phonograph, which Spillers has taken as a matter of concern, her critical project so to say. The phonographic authorship of Spillers is what will be meditated on by way of "Sophisticated Lady," a balladic ode to the one to whom, in the introductory remark, Duke Ellington refers in the very exact name, the name of the composition. Yes, this Ellingtonian composition, in making reference to and revering the sophisticated lady, despite the originary inscription of the context, becomes different when it comes to Mingus. Ellington does not make clear who this sophisticated lady is. It is a song of the mysterious figure. By the spirit of the compositional titling alone, it is worth conjuring up, and thus extending this appellative of the sophisticated lady into the figure of Spillers. As such, the mood and the modulation of the discourse change if the sophisticated lady is refigured in this contemporary conjuncture as the figure of thought.

There is no case for contradicting the claim that Spillers is a sophisticated lady. This can even go to all matters beyond everything that has to do with her thought. But the domain is her thought, and this is where this meditation will dwell. Bringing this in touch with Ellingtonian composition as undertaken by Mingus, and as a matter of Spillers's critical thought, is a case in point.

First, on the originary, by way of a reference to sophistication *à la* Ellington, Amiri Baraka (1963: 162) writes: "Duke's sophistication was to a great extent the very quality that enabled him to integrate so perfectly the older blues traditions with the 'whiter' styles of big-band music." By way of refiguring, in the name of sophistication, Mingus takes this Ellingtonian composition with great command and to greater heights. Mingus, revered as the titan on his bass instrument, with he and the bass fused as one, attests to the portrait that Gene Santoro (2000: 32) puts eloquently thus: "The bass became the core of who Charles Mingus was." This is even more apparent in "Sophisticated Lady," which he delivers as an accompanied bass solo through his own re/interpretation by way of making the original to be original again, albeit *otherwise*.

Here, in the writerly practice that Fred Moten (2003) and Alexander Weheliye (2005) formulate as "phonography," there lies the meditation that Spillers takes by means of black critical thought. What can be understood through specific vernacular modalities, in pointed terms, is that Mingus and Spillers undertake an experiment as they both stretch limits, and there is no way that this can be far from the marker that bears anything that comes in the name of sophistication. Also, it is worth stressing that the phonographic authorship does not come as a transcription, but as what Brent Edwards (2017) calls "poetic work," which actually makes the form, formulation, and formation of "Sophisticated Lady" into a different register altogether. What lies in poetic work is the experiment whose intention is generativity. Edwards (2017: 76) writes: "Music as a metaphor seems a necessary mediating element in the process of linguistic transcription." That is why, for Moten (2017: 123), this is "a rupture that phonography underscores." By way of being extended to Spillers, it is the rupture that leads Alexis Gumbs (2016: 63) to note that "the sound of her writing is the quietest dance made to tiptoe over the ocean."

If this is writing, or if writing is anything to go by, Moten (2017) states, it is what is perceived as what delays or defers – the suspense of immediacy. This creates generativity in the hold, the actualization of freedom even if it is not within reach at that particular time.

Mingus's "Sophisticated Lady" is the live performance delivered at Cornell University in 1964 and Fumi Okiji (2018: 74) gives its expository account thus: "There is an imperative in jazz to play a standard – that is, to tell a story – within one's own particularities, both physical and perspectival. A musician uses the tools at his or her disposal, often turning apparent limitations to advantage." Cornell University is that same institution where Spillers will teach a few decades later and also, now recently, frequently visits as a guest scholar. By tying "Sophisticated Lady" to Spillers, it remains clear that what is form, formulation, and formation concerns the materiality of the phonography, which, to Weheliye (2005), is the equation of language with "pure form."

Since Mingus makes his aesthetic deliverance by means of refiguration and where things do not stay the same, what if, by way of reimagining *otherwise*, "Sophisticated Lady" cannot only be extended to listening to Spillers's black modern text, but to take the composition as the ode to the figure of the phonographic author who keeps black life alive even in the midst of its denial? What would it mean for Mingus to say "sophisticated lady" to Spillers? In this composition, which is the re-interpretation of the jazz standard, it is therefore apt to extend the prerogative that Spillers is the sophisticated lady. By this radical gesture, the articulation is not reducible to the level of the spectacle, but emphasizes the sound and text that comes from "Sophisticated Lady" as the standard composition of the black modern text. This is where the figure of the phonographic author pronounces and accentuates itself.

What is it that marks the "Sophisticated Lady" *qua* Spillers? The way in which phonographic authorship is invented has traces that result from aesthetic markings of the black vernacular, which to Houston Baker (1984: 3) are in the open circuit of a "more sophisticated form of verbal art." The engagement of Spillers with Mingus's work bears the ascription of what might be termed sophisticated music. In this radically generative gesture, Alexis Gumbs (2016: 58) amplifies it to say "she rebrowns her spirit." This is the inventive act, the inventory of the modes of phonographic authorship, the spirit rebrowned as not bowing to what lactifies it to whiteness. That spirit rebrowned stands to refuse to become milky. Clearly, Spillers's spirit is ante/antilactification. There stands sophistication, and this is the rebrowning of the spirit as Gumbs notes. What is in this music that Spillers's spirit has invested through her sophistication? It is worth pausing here, and dwelling briefly with Baraka:

> Music, as paradoxical as it might seem, is the result of thought. It is the result of thought perfected at its most empirical, *i.e.*, as *attitude* and *stance*. Thought is largely conditioned by reference; it is the result of consideration or speculation against reference, which is largely arbitrary. (Baraka 1963: 152)

There is no miss here of what Baraka hits at – sophisticated music. Music performed by blacks is nothing that can be claimed to be unlettered, as the racist tropes have been banally propagated and stereotypically internalized. The sophistication comes with ways of thinking about the world and, so to state, music is composed from those ways of thinking, that lived experience. Thus, this is not reducible to the raw ways that are static, but what Baraka shows as the changing force of this music and how its innovators changed it.

In this sophistication, according to Baker (1984), there is that intertextual matter, which can even be defined as textual or even meta-textual. Also, it is worth stating that the condition of black life is what brought textuality into being and phonographic authorship into "an unlimited play" (Baker 1984: 11). The disfigurement of sophistication of Spillers is not a matter of misidentification, but the rightful attributes that come from sophisticated vernacularistic modes, which not only conjure up sublime registers but bring the phonograph to the affective registers, whose expression is that of bent tongues. Here, as Nathaniel Mackey (2018: 40) notes, "language is thematized and acted upon." The resultant aspect of this is how experimentation is not only embarked on but sustained and pushed to the limit. This, which even has relevance to Mingus's "Sophisticated Lady," comes into being as refiguring, attending to "broken speech" and "speech breaking"; to Mackey (2018: 42), both work to break new ground – "the prospect and promise of a new beginning." This amounts to the originary force that, then, becomes the first site of language – the utterance of original tongues.

The matter here is that Mingus's "Sophisticated Lady" is not outside form, but in the break (Moten 2003). Edwards (2017: 60) amplifies it: "There is no 'pure' matter that would somehow be outside form, or without form."

Extending this from where Ellington left, it is worth attending to Moten (2003: 24), who submits: "[this is] no originary configuration of attributes but an ongoing shiftiness, a living labor of engendering to be organized in its relation to politico-aesthesis." With this, it is clear that the idea of purity is under strain, even meaningless. The resistance to be held is what "Sophisticated Lady" is. It is a composition of political resistance. Mingus makes his politico-aesthetic tongue directly pointed, through thoughtful ways that bear the mark of sophistication itself.

But here is the moment that is of interest with regard to "Sophisticated Lady" and its being a matter of life and death. About the bomb scare at Yale University, in the year 1972, Claudia Pierpont (2010) recounts how all people were evacuated for their safety, and everybody got out except for Mingus, who held onto his bass on stage. That event was the benefit concert by black musicians for the African American music academy and the source of the bomb scare was someone who was not happy with the idea, and wanted Yale University to remain a white enclave. The reason for the scare was to make sure that the concert did not happen, and the status quo remained. Mingus, in his radical insistence on and for freedom, remained on stage and refused to be evacuated. He is quoted as saying: "If I'm going to die, I am ready. But I'm going out playing 'Sophisticated Lady'" (Pierpont 2010). These are the words of someone who is ready to face death while playing Ellington's composition. This, according to Pierpont, made Ellington, who was there among the evacuated crowd, wear a smile on his face in admiration of Mingus's unimaginable courage. It is known that Ellington tried always to be apolitical, but Mingus was political proper and did not mince words against any form of dehumanization. Speaking against death, Mingus did so in the name of "Sophisticated Lady." It is in its name that he pledged the end of his life. So be it! Yes, in the name of "Sophisticated Lady."

The aesthetic labor that Mingus performs is ante/antipurity – that is to say, contrapuntal labor. Santoro (2000: 67) augments: "His complex life seemed to demand new forms of expression." It is on this motif that what is set to come into being is what has all to do with generativity's force. In Spillers's writerly practice, what is bearing the name of sophistication itself, the criticism of purity, her phonographic authorship is the contrapuntal nature in a sense of what Tina Campt (2017) calls the sound that conjures up sounds of the everyday life. What is radically insisted on in Spillers, for Campt (2017: 45), is "the hum of utopian dreams and diasporic aspiration." There is the sublime side and sight of "Sophisticated Lady," whose minor keys lower frequencies, which, for Campt, have a bearing on what is seen and its resonance. "Sophisticated Lady" might be deemed to be a song that is all about the beauty of the doll-like lady, but what is key to note, following Campt (2017: 32), is how she "exceeds the regulatory function." The creation of the life that is worth living is what Spillers is all about. Therefore, the composition, "Sophisticated Lady," under the radical penning of black life, is what exceeds the regulative capture, the limit as it were. Spillers's phonographic authorship is the dissenting gesture where sound and words merge. In Mingus's artistic spirit, radically bold and explicitly expressive, Spillers comes to capture the sound of blackness. This is the grammar that erupts in ways that are sophisticated in the sense of the title of the composition itself.

Here, what emerges, even still, are what Mackey (2018) calls "sound-words," which stand for the denotative nature of phonography. But form is not fixed, it is alterable, and such alteration can, as Edwards (2017) notes, alter the content. By interfacing Mingus and Spillers, the work of refiguration is put into practice in order to meditate on the composition "Sophisticated Lady" and the phenomenon called sophisticated lady. The former is Mingus, and the latter is Spillers. This, by way of altering the content, brings writing to the domain that Edwards ruptures as what is theoretical and what also is writerly. Here is Edwards (2017: 9): "The music, one might say, possesses a native intelligence before and beyond any writing."

"Sophisticated Lady," when taken in the manner of Mingus's refigured deliverance, invites new modes of listening and inhabiting the world. This is not breaking with Ellingtonian balladic muse, but re-elaborating his composition, and translating it to another tongue – that vernacularity as the language of the black modern text that Spillers shifts and uplifts by modes of phonographic authorship. Mingus's "Sophisticated Lady," Santoro (2000: 281) claims, "was jarringly out of tune." There is nothing that can bear the word "sophisticated" in that the song should be in tune to even at least get that mention. Much worse by far, it is, to the extreme, "jarring." In Mingus's hands, Santoro believes, "Sophisticated Lady" was botched. The issue of whether or not to contend with the merits of this claim, perhaps to note what is in tune and what is out of tune, in so far as Mingus's sophisticated music is concerned, is a debatable matter. And that, of course, is informed by the spectrum of sensibility and its auditory taste. In his bass command, in his provocative articulation, what is jarringly sounding out of tune is what can also be regarded as in tune. There lies the issue of sophistication. But this does suggest that Santoro's claim is worth being examined further, not in terms of its merits but for understanding the aesthetic merits that are openly debatable in so far as Mingus's sophistication is concerned. Mingus unshackled "Sophisticated Lady" from the genre of the ballad and his rendition was gesturing toward the speaking voice. It is this aesthetic uplift that grammatizes not only the genre, but what makes the Spillerian phonographic authorship see interruption as the trait through which the elevation of language comes into being by way of aesthetic form. The vernacularized form of "Sophisticated Lady" is articulated in what turns out to be the language of many tongues. That is why, under Spillers's pen and spelling, the phonographic authorship of "Sophisticated Lady" is the mapping of the tongue that is not only in motion but in flight.

It is by this call that the encounter between Mingus (sound) and Spillers (text) meet, not on the comparative plane, but by extension of form and thus by rendering any form of inscription to bear rupture. Both Mingus and Spillers are sophisticated in their aesthetic offering and deliverance. They provoke imagination and they embody black social life in ways that not only appeal to respectability politics but to the radical embodiment of re/un/making of the world.

The punctuation of what is expressed is direct. It is clear to whom Mingus is making an ode, and this is delivered in a duet form – that is, "Sophisticated Lady," as the name of the composition that is delivered in a sophisticated form, thus becomes a formation of the figure of the phonographic author. "Sophisticated Lady" is the aesthetic deliverance, the beauty that must touch ears that will do just anything to care to listen. Its rich history, stemming from Ellingtonian literary genius, is obviously telling. Edwards (2017: 88) writes: "It is well known that Duke Ellington based a number of his compositions on literary sources." Here is an explicit encounter, the animation of phonographic authorship. Ellington, as the figure that Mingus revered, as Spillers reveres Mingus, is something worthy of noting and narrating. This, in many ways, is remarkably the site of what Edwards sees as "telling tales." When these tales are told, they invite different forms of listening that are attuned to the *otherwise*. There is no singular understanding of what the effect of Mingus's rendition of "Sophisticated Lady" is. Like many jazz standards, it is fraught with mystery. It can even be said that it also signifies the myth and legend. But one thing is for sure, it moved the audience there at Cornell University in 1964. Even after that event, and the recorded sound as the capture of what happened there, the song will still hit those who have their ears tuned on the phonograph. Also, it will hit them differently depending on their modes of reception and sensibilities. Those who care to listen, first, in this instance, are, by way of being refigured in this encounter, this radical conjuncture, Mingus and Spillers. They are sophisticated and they are the primal listeners. Okiji (2018: 75) gives an apt formulation of the two thus: "The storyteller and the jazz musician are listeners." Both are sophisticated listeners. More fundamentally, there is no phonographic authorship outside sophisticated listening. This mode of listening is sustained.

By declaring that the text and context are in a mode of refiguration it is worth stating that "Sophisticated Lady" brings into being the vernacular inscription of black social life where writing about jazz is the quotidian experience. The lettering of black culture is what Spillers delivers with sophistication. The composition of "Sophisticated Lady" comes from Mingus's aesthetic offering and its sounding is the language that speaks to the figure that is not only identifiable – but elevated if not revered.

Mingus, according to Santoro (2000: 38), is there "to improvise life as he did music, to compose his history." This is delivered in sophisticated modes. This is deemed to be, by Santoro, in the realm of "unclassifiable ideas," which are the marker of his breadth and depth. The sophistication of Mingus's thinking causes Santoro (2000: 7) to state: "Everything in his life was an instant cosmic metaphor." What would this be if not having to come into contact with the figure that radically changed things and thus subjected everything, including himself, to critique and, hence, re-examination? The answer lies in the exploratory nature that Mingus undertook in delivering "Sophisticated Lady."

With a deep and solo phrasing, Mingus is, in "Sophisticated Lady," accompanied by Jaki Byard on piano, and this is the grammar that is clear, but words cannot be traced. It is a sensual mystique, and the texture of the piano is as if it is played in a small jazz club filled with the legendary ambiance. "The sound is sometimes visually figured as a certain aural duskiness, smokiness, or huskiness and sometimes characterized, by way of taste and/or touch, as rich and velvety" (Moten 2017: 130). The piano is at the back and the bass on front. Even at the level of audibility, something is going on here, with the command of the bass, its complex rhythms and textures, Mingus is on, firmly plucking those strings. There is the mystical touch of the lower frequencies of the piano played along by Byard. There we have that accompanied solo, with the high frequency of the bass and low frequency of the piano, which keeps things in shape, and makes the ear attend to two separate and yet distinct modes of sounding.

The solo bass line presents itself as a way of peddling on still waters running deep. Is that not, in fact, what is happening when listening to Mingus and Byard? That is the case. That is how what is imagined gets actualized in so far as the bass and piano registers of "Sophisticated Lady" are concerned. It is the phonography of bass lines riding over the piano. The bass is above and the piano below. By means of this compositional arrangement, the effect of what comes to the ear as sophisticated succeeded.

Byard, in his carpet playing, allows Mingus to go all over his soft touches of keys. Even Mingus, by continuing where his forebears left, reveres what is sophisticated and, for him, as a sophisticated musician, he makes pronouncements through his song and wants his audience, listeners, and critics to come to know the sophisticated lady. By attuning the ear to "Sophisticated Lady," it is as if there are two solos that are played in different phonographs, if not geographies. When each channel is imaginatively closed, Mingus's bass and Byard's piano registers are like two songs, which, on their own, can be titled "Sophisticated Lady." What is vernacularized by both Mingus and Byard independently of each other is nothing that is short of sophistication itself. The ear, listening to the song as it is, the solo and its accompaniment, presents sophistication in having to come to terms with two textures of sonic expression. Mingus is fast paced while Byard is steady. There are various notes with Mingus, while that is not the case with Byard. One thing about "Sophisticated Lady" is the thought that there will be a chorus joining. That, as an anticipation, is to be forever suspended. And the song, as it is, becomes beautiful and there is a forgetting of that anticipation. It can be forgotten that Johnny Coles on trumpet, Clifford Jordan on tenor sax, Dannie Richmond on drums, and Eric Dolphy on alto sax and baritone clarinet are on stage when this Mingus–Byard deliverance takes place. It can even be, while lingering outside this anticipation, a long song. But it never becomes that, as Mingus ends it, but it is never a short song either; it is a fulfilling song.

Only the bass is doing the talking and it, with the accompanying piano that commands silence, makes the song so touching. Mingus's bass lines, his being all over the bass – neck, upper bout and C bout right down to crossing the bridge, the word uttering of what Moten (2003: 45) puts as "a kind of nonverbal writing: transparent or instrumental, uninflected by the transformations of a buzz-growl extension, bending whistle, hummm" and, in relation to the moment of Mingus's uttering this "hummm," this causes the audience to respond with tinged and short mirth.

> The double bass mumbles and groans, but it is also able to chuckle, twitter, and scream. Mingus, aided by his considerable abilities as a vocalist, tailor makes an approach that plays to these qualities. Along with a display of dexterity across the range of the instrument, he utilizes vocal-like articulation – juxtaposing his bebop with blues-imbued speech. (Okiji 2018: 74)

It is after hitting those three notes below the bridge that Mingus makes the "hummm" utterance. The lady to whom Mingus refers as sophisticated must have struck a chord in Mingus's compositional imagination and there the song was birthed as "Sophisticated Lady." This is the lady on whom Mingus muses and that, by way of an ode, is something that comes from a place of love. Undeniably, the utterance "hummm," the nonverbalized word, says a lot with respect to the sophisticated lady. Mingus loves the sophisticated lady. The sensibility and sentimentality that come with "Sophisticated Lady" as a musical text demand attention, and it is Spillers's meditation where *all things love*, and *all things black life*, come to rupture in order to actualize what should be unfolding. This is the heart and formation, sophistication as it were.

It is clear that it is ladies who are responding to this utterance. The end of "Sophisticated Lady" goes down well, and the end of this accompanied solo spans the entire track duration, plucking the bass below the bridge, Mingus brings the song to an end by saying "hummm" after the last note, again below the bridge, which invites a thunderous applause. This "hummm" can be extended to what Okiji (2018: 79) formulates as "an improvisation of sound, word, music, and meaning." This "hummm" is beyond linguistic capture.

> There is a play between blunt designation and indescribable precision. Raw sound may slip into word and music, becoming music and word to varying degrees. Chewed up words and corrupted musical phrases allow us to share what we were unable to share in plain language. (Okiji 2018: 79)

This, as a matter of language, is another language in that what is pure is invented to accent other modes of expression. What is unsayable is said, and what is said is the unsayable – the critique of purity if it is imposed on form. So, what is pure form lies in having to be articulated "outside, below, and beyond the structures of discourse." So, here, the phonographic authorship of the black modern text is in the mode of what Moten (2018b) articulates as composition and decomposition. Accordingly, phonography, as the study of black life, is a different accent and access, is the way in which black life makes itself audible. It is the composition and decomposition because:

> This is sound mediated by a kind of technology, sound irreducible to words, to speech; bodily presence is cut and augmented by a technological irruption, by something on the order of an invasion of an interior instantiated by that interior, or by the outside that it has taken in. The shameful notice or notation or excess of notation that marks the material irruption of our presence to ourselves is given in/as sound. (Moten 2018b: 51)

The phonograph, according to Weheliye (2005: 29), by its being the capture of "feeling sounds in writing," makes the composition and decomposition of "Sophisticated Lady" to be the sounding and writing of – and as – technology. Writing assumes the status of a recorded sound and, in terms of the musical deliverance, those who are listening to the phonograph encounter what Mingus did live (the latter would not have been known had it not been recorded). The repetition of what was recorded can be, in a form of a record, what is played, paused, rewound, forwarded, dubbed, stopped – and, if need be, repeated. This is because, as Okiji notes, the jazz record is, in itself, a limit. Okiji (2018: 89) avers: "Jazz records are undeniably indispensable, but as a document of the creative process, they are inadequate." Here, the disappearance of the creative process is subjected to the mechanics and technologies of the studio.

> Listening to recordings is the first and primary activity in jazz musicians' pedagogy. Records hold an irreconcilable contradiction in that they help sustain a tradition they are unable to reproduce in their medium, a tradition defined by incompletion, open-endedness, expansive or suspended notions of time, uncertainty … Jazz work is not what is reproduced in records. Studio recordings, to varying degrees, fabricate the jazz work of performance, plays, rehearsal, and practice. The prosperity that comes with them robs the music of a certain readiness to own "failure." The prospect of listening, both during the production process and after release, unseats the priority of "willingness to fail" as musicians move toward the desire for documents that will stand up to close, repeated, structural scrutiny. (Okiji 2018: 90)

What Okiji shows is, in terms of the phonographic material, the aspect of being polished and sanitized – what she calls the fetishized jazz work. Even the recorded live performance is, according to Okiji (2018: 93), what can bear "significant disparity between the jazz studio recording and live jazz." Weheliye (2005) rightfully states that the sonic recordings are the means rather than the end of the record. In other words, it is all that has to do with technology and its modes of it proliferating by means of reproduction. That is why the jazz record is "jazz being documented" (Okiji 2018: 90). And, "Sophisticated Lady" as the jazz record, and dwelling in the place of jazz standard collections, is the work of jazz, which, to Okiji, is the potential of refiguring itself as the work of jazz as long as it is not the singularity of the hegemon. By way of countering and dissolving the singularity of the hegemon, the phonographic experience and literariness are articulated by Moten thus:

> This is to say that the condition of possibility of the reval-
> orization of sound is that its new phonographic medium makes
> possible – by way of itself as medium or as the medium of a
> medium, the vehicle of sound; and by way of repetitive listening
> which it allows – a more proximate relation of the experience of
> music to its essence as writing. Sound comes back but only by
> way of its graphic overwriting, underwriting, *Ur*-writing. The
> phonograph enables the illusory recovery of an architrace. At
> the same time, the vagaries and vulgarities of the visual are held
> off or back by a phonography whose condition of possibility and
> whose end is the illusory recovery of the essential literary – and
> thus essentially visual – experience. (Moten 2018b: 121)

What is the form, formulation, and formation of sophistication that concerns this intervention if not what to Ronald
Judy (2020: 49) is a "truer" self, which (re)presents itself in
its "distinctive actual capacities and expressions free from
the white gaze" and from its point of view? This poesis and,
for Saidiya Hartman (2019a), is the site and citation of black
capacity. The origin of this poesis not only lies in creation
just for its worded sake, but the insistence that pushes the
margins in order for sophistication to emerge. This poesis
in black lies in Spillers writing a phonographic essay, which,
by way of a beginning, it is evident that the woke is to go to
the site and cite the ongoingness of black life. The site and
citation in composing this book is in sermons, poems, fiction,
polemic, argument, music, art, pamphlets, letters, and many
textualities (Spillers 1994). More pressingly, Spillers (1987:
68) marks this sophistication as "a rupture and a radically
different kind of cultural continuation." Spillers presents
what Moten (2003) calls the "new analytic" and this is what
is vernacularity, which is unhooking from the present and
considering what does not yet exist. This new analytic is the
expansion and engages with the creative process who invents.
This is the creation and invention of the known and the
unknown, the input and input that is expanded and everything is about refiguring. The phonographic authorship is the

new and old of the raw material to work with and this is the new analytic. There is nothing composite, and refiguring of what exists, the ongoingness of black life is the new analytic. For Mingus and Spillers are making jazz to be what is directing what is charged to change and overturning what is commonly held, and imprinting the new analytic, using what is done and repurposing it differently, and that, to Moten (2003), is the break. This is black radicalism. "In this sense, black radicalism is (like) black music" (Moten 2003: 24).

Discoursing Sophistication

Spillers's sophistication at the epistemic level is, by the way she thinks and writes, what is not only unique, but what is on the level of its own. This is not at that level of luxury but, rather, being in the pressure cooker, which bursts all things and that even signifies the denial of black life. It is under these conditions that even Mingus refigured "Sophisticated Lady" as the reality that will continue to be the generative site of black life. Here lies the problematic of the double *qua* production. This is the production of sophistication under duress and denial. The production of the work of such a kind is sophistication. A sophisticated lady is engaged in a sophisticated episteme that is denied its canonicity. For such canon formation to come into being, as Judy (1993) states, there should be that "(dis)formation" that becomes the form, formulation, and formation of a different kind. It is the disruption of what has been colonially legible but what is, in form, formulation, and formation – ante/anti-colonial. The sophistication of (dis)forming is the way in which Spillers writes phonography in order to counter the totality of the American canon. That is why, for Judy, this (dis)forming is, in its radical protocol, what interrupts in order to make space. This is the epistemic project of those who are denied, and Judy makes it clear that it is a case, which in particular is for everything whose agenda is proposing and actualizing the ways of thinking differently. It is a mark of this difference that will bring a refiguration of things, black life as it were.

The creation of the world, one which is supposed to be different from the one that both Mingus and Spillers inhabit, signifies what is written in the form of what Judy refers to as a form of literacy, what will be read through the sophistication of the very idea of literariness. If jazz is literature, which is true, as Edwards (2017) states, Mingus wrote a different form of literariness, whose best trait is the departure from the fact. This is the resistance to the empiricist closure and its factual fetishism. Again, noting Judy's (dis)forming, Edwards (2017: 4) argues that "what is misremembered and misconstrued can be the source of formal innovation." It is only by doing things in a different way, the departure that takes a journey on a different way – toward destination unknown. This, as is obvious to Spillers (1994), who sets jazz to literariness, bears the mark of sophistication. The materialization of vernacularity is made clear and manifest by Mingus and Spillers, without their obsessing about legibility's incorporation and closure. At stake here is what refuses to be legible, but the work of writing, whose vernacularity is the work whose form, formulation, and formation is under Judy's mark of (dis)forming. What haunts both Mingus and Spillers is, drawing from Judy (1993: 100), "the paramount danger of thinking." It is from this danger that rupture originates by having been imagined and, therefore, actualized. So, it can be said that both Spillers and Mingus are thinking dangerously. The contemplation of sophistication has to do with creating the world by putting themselves in danger because, by thinking outside any bounds, they are doing so dangerously.

Before Spillers there is a sophisticated musician who composes "Sophisticated Lady" and Mingus takes after him, to sophisticate the ante/anti-colonial sensibilities of all her existentially committed forebears. Surely, this is the marker of sophistication itself. Therefore, by way of rupture, the refiguration of a discourse to be exact, "Sophisticated Lady" as extended to Spillers is what Weheliye (2005) would mark as being summoned by the phonographic record. If everything is, at the level of form, formulation, and formation, made to be ephemeral, yet it is captured for its permanence, then, phonography is the site of investigation where Spillers is rightfully located as the sophisticated lady.

What Spillers embodies is the black female image that Selamawit Terrefe (2018) writes about, who is the figure who deals with the erasure of such a figure. By claiming sophistication, Terrefe points to violent fantasies that are there to ruin black life. In the midst of this – Spillers is the sophisticated lady who structures black life. Sophistication is what goes deep, as it unpacks what is the edifice of antiblackness – Spillers is "the black woman as the arbiter of Blackness itself" (Terrefe 2018: 126). What comes to "Sophisticated Lady" is what, by way of Spillers's hermeneutics is what extends to "the spectacular." Spillers is such, she bears a mirror, she is a reflection and to Mingus what comes to vision is what he sees – a sophisticated lady. The specular is revered and the ode is extended to her, and the sophistication of Spillers's writing mirrors black social life. Her sophistication is also the language and discourse – the epistemic intervention that grammatizes black social life. The specular in Mingus's vision is not a shadow, it is a sophisticated lady – seeing her for who she is. This is the lady who is not the object of sadistic desire, which is objectified in order to be consumed by the racist gaze. In the perpetual ruins that come as the result of racist objectification – the mark of dehumanization and death – there is a song that comes to testify on the subject of formation and its politicization, whose radicality is nothing but the insistence on living even in the midst of clutches of death; this is what marks Spillers's writerly practice. By statement and standing, Spillers is a sophisticated lady who objects to racist objectification. That is to say, the sophistication of Spillers lies in her giving it her all for the life that is lived in the name of freedom. Even if that freedom is not there, being in relentless pursuit of it is the mark of sophistication.

Moreover, the sophisticated lady is not the one who is seen through objectified lenses, a fetish of racist eros and accompanied rapaciousness. The body that is structured by these diabolical senses, what is always denied subjecthood, its fixity, is what will deny any attribution of beauty to black womanhood. There is no begging for sophistication. It is there and it is pronouncement as such. There is no conjuring up that there is a "Sophisticated Lady" as everything is a given testimony – for what they really are. The defacing and disfigurement of the sophisticated lady is what Mingus and Spillers (just like the Ellingtonian original and originary aesthetic deliverance) stand against this ontological crisis. Terrefe (2018: 136) declares: "This crisis is an encounter without a relation that is the material and mimetic encounter between a non-self and a barred encounter with the black female imago that represents one's ontological negation." The sophisticated lady is the figure of refusal. It is the refusal to be "effectively buried in the *mis-en-scéne* of racial intrusion, misrecognized as Other" (Terrefe 2018: 137). As if drawing from Mingusque muses of "Sophisticated Lady," Terrefe (2018: 137) is on point to note: "One must comment on ethical, political and scopic orientation toward the Black woman's absented imago, her suffering under erasure." What does it mean to be a sophisticated lady while being absented? In what ways is this sophistication maintained under such conditions of brutality? What is given, exactly, in the name of this sophistication?

The form, formulation, and formation of what is phonographic authorship is the mark and trace that embodies Spillers's lettered spirit. The re-articulation of a discourse is, for Spillers, what comes from the everyday practice of black life. Here, it is worth reaching for Saidiya Hartman (2019b), who calls this form of writing liner notes and whose distinction is nothing but a riot. Here, the authoring that accompanies the phonographic record bears the writing that refuses to submit to the closures and compressions that choke life out of black life. The revelation of sophistication is carried together by Mingus and Byard, and this is held firm by Spillers who, by way of phonographic authoring, shows how the vernacularity of blackness is the aesthetic deliverance not only of talent, but the radical commitment to existential freedoms. According to Hartman (2019b: 1), Spillers's vernacularity, its uncontested sophistication, is "an effort to articulate the conceptual rigors of black women's everyday life and ordinary use." This is a result of having to find the grammar in riot and Hartman qualifies that by calling for the way of making and doing the world, and which, by radical insistence, must be recalibrated. This is sophistication at best because what is calibrated ceases to be *what was* and it is the state of *what is* a matter of complexity. In accounting for sophistication, Hartman (2019b: 1) calls for the vernacularity of "a grammar of (not) being in the world" and that being informed by the radical practices of black life. In locating Spillers as the figure of the black maternal *qua* "Sophisticated Lady," Hartman (2019b: 1) writes in her liner notes thus: "The stark outline of the predicament is that the one who makes a home for others in the world finds herself outside the parameters of the human, not seen and never regarded, excluded and negated." The sophisticated lady who, in her blackness and thus denied being, continues to make the world. This is the figure of injury. At the level of being objectified, she is not seen, nor regarded, and negated. This ontological violation is what animates the very idea of sophistication. Is Spillers (1987: 65) not right to declare: "Let's face it. I am a marked woman, but not everybody knows my name." Here is what darts right at the heart of Mingus's "Sophisticated Lady." This is the lady who is, by virtue of her blackness, marked. These marks are violent inscriptions and what is seen is not her being but her corporeality. In an antiblack world, to see the black, as Lewis Gordon (1995) notes, is to see the black – nothing but black – that is, hypervisibility. The sophisticated lady is the one who is not seen as human by the racist gaze but the object to be consumed by it – figural and real. By calling for the reflection to come into being, Spillers vernacularizes her ontological erasure, and this is the pain that has been suffered by other black maternal figures before and with her, including the ones who are yet to assume this status.

The name of the black maternal and her offspring is what is yet to be unknown, and the systematic erasure will continue to abound – the markings that will make themselves legible to mute any form of vernacularity and to ensure that no sophistication emerges from the black. But, then, the sophistication that Spillers brings to the fore is not that of having been exempted from the violence that has marked the figure of the black maternal since capture, subjection, and continued structural violence, whose racist mechanics and machinations are nothing but defacing and disfigurement. It is in the midst of this dehumanization that Mingus composed "Sophisticated Lady" and Spillers embodied that sophistication, and thus waxed lyrical about, even in the absence of "symbolic integrity" and pathologization, the vernacularization of what is phonographically recorded. It is important to note that the black maternal whole material is sophistication itself. But this is forever denied. But actualization happens anyway. Hartman (2019a: 2) lyrically scripts in a liner note motif thus: "Hortense Spillers explicates the gift and impossibility of the black maternal ..." The aesthetics of what is impossible is possibility. Even if this possibility is denied, the epistemic matter, in practice, comes to be what the black ceases to be.

Spillers bears sophistication when she unmasks the forces that disfigure the figure of the black maternal by mobilizing the vernacularity and inaugurates grammars of existential freedom. Moten (2018a: 95) puts it clearly to say: "In the space that jargon opens ... the rest is what is left for us to say, the rest is what is left for us to do, in the broad and various echoes of that utterance, our attunement to which assures us that we know all we need to know about freedom." The phonographic authorship, to Spillers (1987: 68), "offers a praxis and a theory, a text for living and for dying, and a method for reading both through their diverse mediations." What is this if not the work of a sophisticated lady? This work is as such in that it is the eruption and interruption. This is the sophistication that comes with understanding liner notes that Hartman (2019b) prepares and presents for the riot. It is, according to Moten (2018a: 94), "the kind of narrative wherein knowledge of freedom is given to us and for us." This is the riot that is there for rupture. Its vernacularity presents matters that have to do with the condition of being-black-in-an-antiblack-world, where everything that has to do with sophistication is erased, denied, masked, interdicted, defaced, disfigured, corrupted, broken, and disposed of when it comes to the black. Well, it is clear that Mingus and Spillers enunciate sophistication without any confirmatory anticipation, or paternalistic validation, or pretentious compliments. It is sophistication as it were. The sophisticated lady is what Mingus's song is and it is what Spillers's text is. This song and text stand for the embodiment of phonography. This is what Hartman (2019b: 1) calls "existence in a minor key," and which, without any contest, is the textual form, formulation, and formation of Spillers's phonographic authorship. In this phonographic authorship, by liner notes for a riot, Hartman (2019b: 2) writes: "There is care and beauty too." This is apt in Mingus's composition. Sophistication comes as the result of care and beauty. That is why, in the way it is grammatized, it is through the phonographic authorship whose tongue is nothing but sophistication. So, to say vernacularity *qua* Spillerian phonographic authorship is to say sophistication.

It is in this articulation that, by rupture, where sophistication encounters and is extended to sophistication – Mingus *qua* Spillers – what emerges is the animation of composition *qua* decomposition. Form, formulation, and formation of phonographic authorship, a textual sounding of sorts and accents, access what Moten (2018b: 159) argues is "a reinaugural rupture." Mingus's composition is rupture and Spillers's decomposition is rupture. This is not only the figure of the double or what is made to have the redoubling effect. Instead, Moten directs attention to interruption as what, as a form of interruption, creates form, formulation, and formation in that interruption.

Is sophistication what is free from interruption? Well, the sophisticated lady is the figure that caught Mingus's attention and that made an impression on him to extend an ode to her. The figure of the maternal, through the acts of giving life, will always interrupt the forces that deny this life. This interruption is the intervention that the figure of the black maternal always makes. It is after having learned from the figure of the black maternal, whose central role for black life is form, formulation, and formation that Mingus goes on to audaciously audition his music to the audience who, by way of listening, should not interrupt him while he, by playing his music, interrupts their sensibilities. This motif stems from the fact that he has something important to say and here he tells a story through his bass lines by means of "Sophisticated Lady."

Text and Tongue

The Spillerian text and tongue is the sophistication that demands the impossible and this, for Hartman (2019b), is rooted in the existential struggle that refuses to submit to strictures and closures that come in the name of the impossible. This is the impossibility that is erected for there to be nothing in so far as the black insatiably demands. Whatever the black demands are is deemed impossible and it is in this impossibility that Mingus and Spillers phonographically script the vernacular of the impossible, one that is even impossible, but yet it is lived *as possible*. Hartman insists on the possibility that is deemed impossible because it is the language that, in demanding the possible, is made impossible by antiblackness. Hartman engages in this insistence of possibility as the mode of black radicality. The rupture of sophistication comes as having confronted the impossible. As Hartman (2019b: 2) states, this is the "study inside the enclosure." Those who are denied sophistication are obviously denied their humanity and they are also deemed not worthy of anything that is in the name of sophistication. But, still, this is the false standard of antiblackness that both Mingus and Spillers shutter. Both possess sophistication with both hands. As a direct reference to Spillers's sophistication, Hartman (2019b: 2) makes the argument that "the black femme is a figure and vessel of contemplation." More important to ask is: What, then, happens in this contemplation? The vernacularity that comes is the folding and unfolding of the phonographic authorship as the "runaway tongue," which to Hartman (2019a) is the origin of those fugitive grammars that embody "resistant orality." This is the resistance that is all in the name of the sophistication that

Mingus and Spillers contemplate and embody, respectively or otherwise.

The black creative intellectual, according to Spillers, is the figure of sophistication. Mingus is, according to Spillers, the black creative intellectual. In fact, it will be important to outline briefly the song titles of Mingus's compositions from their elegant complexity and provocation, to say the least. These compositions run from the graspable to the ungraspable, the sacred to the profane – that is, to all manner of the moderate to the extreme. Nicole Rustin-Pascal (2017: 22) argues that "Mingus walks the line between what is real and what is imagined, what is documentable and what is laughable." Before stating these compositions, by way of a detour, it will be important to name a few albums before the compositional tracks composed therein. Just randomly, not only to make a case, but to state the obvious about Mingus's genius, which qualifies him as a creative intellectual, here they are as Mingus identifies himself – to name a few: *Mingus Ah Um* (1959), *Charles Mingus Presents Charles Mingus* (1960), *Mingus Dynasty* (1960), and *Mingus, Mingus, Mingus, Mingus* (1964). Then, also, interestingly titled albums like *Pithecanthropus Erectus* (1956), *The Clown* (1957), *Blues & Roots* (1960), *Oh Yeah* (1960), *The Black Saint and the Sinner Lady* (1963), *Tonight at Noon* (1964), *Let My Children Hear This Music* (1972), *Changes Two* (1975), *Three or Four Shades of Blue* (1975), and *Something Like a Bird* (1980). Then, more to the interesting part, here is the sampled collage of title tracks: "Sophisticated Lady," "Hog Callin' Blues," "Fables of Faubus," "Orange was the Color of Her Dress, Then Blue Silk," "Black Bats and Poles," "Haitian Fight Song," "Lock 'Em Up," "Wrap Your Troubles in Dreams," "Better Git Hit In Your Soul," "Perdido," "Wednesday Prayer Meeting," "Hora Decubitus," "The Shoes of the Fisherman's Wife Are Some Jive Ass Slippers," "Memories of You," "Slop," "E's Flat Ah's Flat Too," "Flamingo," and, more interestingly, to say the least, "All the Things You Could Be By Now If Sigmund Freud's Wife Was Your Mother" which is the ante of Spillers's famous essay, which is the phonographic authorship proper – "All the Things You Could Be By Now If Sigmund Freud's Wife Was Your Mother: Psychoanalysis and Race." But it is clear here that both Mingus and Spillers were engaged in psychoanalysis and from a Freudian touch, whose meditation is not a blush but a crunch, as everything is pushed to the limits, so that there is rupture. Here are two black figures in America engaged in the phonography of psychoanalysis in black. For Mingus, the composition, from his announcement to the imagined audience, the lyrics of the song mean nothing. But Spillers takes this up, and to the different destiny, that departure from/off the fact as per the formulation Edwards (2017) put to the fore. By this, it remains clear that what Mingus states as nothing is not a closure, but the opening. For there is "if," and that calls for the imagination of what things, could one be, if Sigmund Freud's wife was, of course, the mother. Spillers takes this title seriously without modification and re-elaborates it with a subtitle that presents the problematic of race and psycho-analysis. It is interesting how Spillers concludes the essay by reflecting on Mingus.

Mingus is the black creative intellectual and his prolific and very innovative textual formation by being a composer lends him credence. What more about his own fictive autobiography *Beneath the Underdog*? Is it not worth underlining that this is the autobiography written by the jazz musician himself, with his own pen? Is this not the authoritative text that has marks of the brilliant author? In fact, in all his given talents, as a composer, bassist, critic, essayist, writer, conductor, and thespian, Mingus is the figure *extraordinaire*. A lot has been lettered on his erratic outburst, violence, womanizing, and all excess embodied in one person, who battled with demons and angels of this world. But his aesthetic standing stood erect, no matter what. So, Mingus is a black creative intellectual. To state, as a matter of record, "Sophisticated Lady" originates from black creative intelligence. According to Spillers (1994), the black creative intellectual is the figure that defines his or her self-in-writing as the result of reflection and reflex in crisis and taking a radically committed stance. For Mingus (1971), jazz is true work, true music – "true jazz." This means, being a black creative intellectual, his soul must be straight and not stray. Being right up, standing upright (the upright man and the upright bass) all things are erect. This is a presence, a statement, a testament. For Mingus is a figure who is structured in and by crisis, which, in its existential structure, is the denial of black life. All there is for the black creative intellectual is to push boundaries. It is to burst the bubble of the given life-word.

Pushing boundaries and rethinking what they do is how, by pushing things to new territories, black creative intellectuals work on that mode of going somewhere else and doing things otherwise. In pushing the limits of their creativity, both Mingus and Spillers become the materiality of the phonograph. To discover what works, they are engaged in the familiar and the weird. By pushing boundaries, and there is that border of the possible, the spectrum is not clear and known. It is dwelling on the agonizing form of creating things and taking a risk every time because the work of the creative intellectual is confronting failure and doing the opposite. The reality of having to fail, and the confrontation of that failure, is what pushed the sophistication that comes with the black creative intellectual. The degree of failure in Mingus while composing, and in Spillers's writing, is the creative process that shows how pushing boundaries is something that is seen from inside-out. There is, in sophistication, the perpetual edge to cultivate what is to be done and, for Moten, this is the creation that is driven to and by fugitivity, the perpetual move toward, and search for black aurality. This to Moten, is the "freedom drive." This is the drive toward the radical possibility. "This possibility came from the locomotive's drive and thrust, its promise of unrestrained mobility and unlimited freedom" (Baker 1984: 11). The refusal of decadence is the accenting of sophistication. So, in these terms, to say sophistication is to say freedom drive. By black aurality, Moten calls for what he terms expansive, that invagination and imagination – put differently, that "non-determining invitation." Mingus is extending an ode and makes it known that this is the song for the sophisticated lady. The materiality of black aurality is what, for Spillers, stands for clarity about which side the black creative intellectual should take, and thus is the basis through which the work unfolds. The black creative intellectual is a committed intellectual on the freedom drive. This is the figure who acts and, for Mackey (1995), pursues "black liberties," to refigure language in the name of the freedom drive. Everything is active, and so are Mingus and Spillers in their sophistication. This is, notes Ashon Crawley (2016: 88), "making something with a radical potentiality and critical edge." To amplify, Hartman (2019a: 228) is on point when he remarks: "It is the untiring practice of trying to survive to live when you were never meant to survive." The Motenian freedom drive is liberatory. It is the drive that augments sophistication in having to combat an antiblack world.

In an antiblack world, as Spillers (1994: 73) asserts, "the black creative intellectual *ought* to be not only a member in good standing but perhaps among the *first* standing." Reference is being made directly to Mingus; it is indeed true that he is both in *good* and *first* standing. He practiced freedom through his politico-aesthetic pursuits. Crawley (2016: 91) writes: "Each practice, therefore, was likewise a preparation for the possibility of the threat of violation; each practice thus highlights the ways in which interventions always likewise have an aesthetic quality and theoretical underpinning." That, there, is sophistication. And, for the black creative intellectual, it is this standing that is in the name not only of sophistication, but its source, which is the work of the freedom drive. That is why, by this, Spillers (1994) acknowledges the black musical superior degree to the condition of being occasioned and allowed. But it is also true that the freedom drive against exploitation and dehumanization of black musicians has been the crisis that Mingus had to stand up against in explicit political terms. In fact, it is well known. The occasioning and allowing of Mingus and his musical heirs and contemporaries have always been with a greater cost. There has been the infrastructural halt of the freedom drive. But the pursuit of elegance that accents sophistication lies in the practice that births it, its nurturing even.

By proposing a different thought, but what still foregrounds the very concepts of refiguring, Spillers (1994: 114) writes: "At some time, the black creative intellectuals must respond to this aspect of the definition of *siting* on the conceptual object." This is not to say that this conceptual object is the idea of singularity, but it has to meditate on it, and take its ordinariness to be extraordinary. This means, by taking a stance, and being for all good and first standing, the creative intellectual, just like Mingus and Spillers alike, must, by way of refiguring, take sophistication not only as the attribute of corporeality, but the totality of being, where all senses are mobilized through the un/re-making of another world. In music, Mingus took the raw and subjected it to invention. In text, Spillers did the same. By way of phonographic authorship, there is that commitment to what is supposed to be done. This is always, by execution, forever original. Spillers (2017: 96) amplifies it to say: "So in this moment we find ourselves trying to protect creative impulses once again." This is the duty that must be carried not for the sake of sophistication but life itself. That is why for Mingus, as Rustin-Pascal (2017: 5) notes, this is "the continuous examination and reexamination of the self – as part of his creative intellectual labor."

In sum, "Sophisticated Lady" is a standard, a classic – say, connoisseurship. It is a compositional sophistication itself from the Ellingtonian muse right to/through Mingusque requisition. Thus refigured, by way of extending it to Spillerian phonographic authorship, it becomes the rupture of the black modern text. To say Ellington, Mingus, and Spillers, is to say sophistication. It is also to say everything in the name of the black music.

The composition that is rooted in the phonographic authorship takes the form of an alternative take, which proliferates to many other "takes." It is as if it is a gift that says: "Where are the takers?" Since this is the refiguring of the original and making something original out of the original (not a copy of course), the radical commitment is passing the message from one generation to the next. The defiance of genre, the radical gesture of openness, the very idea of what is in the name of the experiment, is the very thing that informs "Sophisticated Lady." And, the way the composition is phonographically authored to be different in coming to Spillers, it is deferred. This is not a matter of being late, of articulating the latest forms, but it is the affinity to the tradition that gave birth to vernacularity, and it being in the mold and hold of blackness, different registers marking another language that has been there in the first place. The materiality of the phonograph cannot be tied to form and content. It is clear how the different installments of "Sophisticated Lady" have moved from Ellington to Mingus, and how they are given a different shape in locating Spillers *as that* sophisticated lady. Sophistication is what vernacularity is. Sophistication is what phonographic authorship is.

Verso

The formulation that is put forth, by means of refiguring, is a discursive intention.

So far, the hesitance of its definitiveness, its totality, its finality, rests in taking generativity seriously by way of marking the end as the beginning. It is, then, worth asking: What does it mean to begin at the end? What is it that lies at the edge of the limit? What are the modes of thinking outside orthodoxy? Considering these propositional questions, in the domain of thought as it were, this is not reducible to the politico-philosophical discourse. It is apparent that the disposition is, however, different. That is what refiguring is. It is the adversative of closure, the advocate of radical openness. That is why, in the imaginary and actuality of black life, matters of discourse, if that is anything to go by, the very thing that this foregoing suite is all about, it is prudent to say things are about to unfold. This is said in the spirit of not claiming any form of the exhaustive absolute, but the beginning of a counter-discourse, if the discourse is in the name of this exhaustive absolute. Where is this counter-discourse if not in black thought? As mentioned, just earlier, it is clear that this is not for dissent's own sake, but what is necessary to do when the claim is that of engaging in black thought. Also, there is no desire to be included in the exclusionary domain of what claims to be discourse proper. Thought has been what has been denied to black life, and this fallacy does not have the absolute traction, as black life is re/thought in deciphering and powerful ways, which make closure not the final word. There is everything of black life after and beyond closure because there is black thought in its different registers.

This suite, by way of its thematization, through the route and even detour of Douglass, Morrison, Spillers, and Mingus, who engaged critical thinkers of the refiguring practice, makes it necessary to claim affinity to what comes in the name of rupture. It is a practice of rupturing enclosure that is the case of this meditation. It is, in other words, a contrarian take in modernity's enclosure, departing from the known, and gesturing toward the *otherwise*; refiguring is rightfully imprinted, not only for its textual and contextual suitability, but also its generative protocols. Both in discourse and everyday black life, the generative protocol is in the name of what is being gestured to and thus enacted in ways that have not been anticipated. That is why there is always this intentioned *otherwise*.

What would it mean to think with and through Douglass, Morrison, Spillers, and Mingus *otherwise*? This has been the intentional motif of this book. It is the radical insistence to radically refuse erasure, and the modes of inscriptions that come in the name of black thought that are refigured. Therefore, what is the norm and form is pushed to the edge. In the hands of Douglass, Morrison, Spillers, and Mingus, black thought is turned into the erudite work of craft and exposition. They make black life to be the site of possibility and they give insights into and about this possibility. This, then, gives a clear sense of what their work is in having to center refiguring. There lies rupture, its unfolding, even.

Clearly, just to punctuate, *Refiguring in Black* is the critical disposition and exposition that is intended to launch different ways of thinking blackness. This is done without prescriptive and decadent enclosures that claim to be the purity and totality of things – say, the last word. However, though, the generative protocols, whose obviousness is the

opening and unbundling of what has been the formulation
of the last word, its closure, thinking blackness has been
the discourse of the *otherwise*. Or, its figure of the double,
where the blackness sees itself in relation to whiteness, this
is obliterated. This decoupling of what burdens blackness,
rendering it the double-face (which is to say the masking
that defaces blackness), the work that is being done, in
the name of refiguration, is what reveals the real face. The
masks must fall. Blackness cannot speak in another name
other than its own. In refiguring, that being the practice of
Douglass in giving the harrowing account of the beating of
Aunt Hester, Morrison rewriting the episteme in arguing for
the Africanistic presence, and Spillers being argued for as the
sophisticated lady through her phonographic authorship of
Mingus's "Sophisticated Lady," it is clear that the matters
that are dealt with here are not far from being propositional.
This is the suite of what is unfolded, what is unfolding, and
what is about to unfold. That is where their richness lies in
that they are germane sites whose insights, which are fundamentally black, make sure that the work of unmasking does
not cease. Everything is on the move and, where things are
being pushed to the edge, as this book shows, unmasking is
a continual act in the name of refiguring.

This suite is not restoring order. Nor is it invested in the
idea of purity, or that uncritical nostalgia of *as things were*.
Rather, it is aimed at creating what is not in the name of the
modern colonial world but a liberated one. This is the work
of freedom, and its construction of the world is the liberated
world. To be invested in black thought, its criticality, is the
work of remaking the world. It is having to depart from the
current conjuncture and bring into being the means through
which reality can be fundamentally changed, and it should be
in its name that there will be ways through which the disposition is fundamentally black. This means taking a stance and
speaking in the name of the discursive re-grounding, where
matters of black thought are what help in principality.

Being rooted in black life, and not flirting with flight from
it, is the principality of having to think about the point of view
and also the worldview of Douglass, Morrison, Spillers, and

Mingus. So, their account of black life is what comes at the greater cost of not only having to narrate what is happening to blacks, but to confront and combat what is happening to blacks. They do so by declaring themselves black and it is in this blackness that they speak in their own name. They own their blackness and, as such, refuse to be seduced into things that will make them disavow their blackness. It is clear from Douglass, Morrison, Spillers, and Mingus that they think, write, and reflect not only on what is in their immediate grasp, but what also surrounds them, and their contrapuntal take is what aims to engender freedom from what aims to render them captive. In exercising their discursive protocols, meditating on matters central to black thought, what is put forth is the work that confronts captivity. Having thought in the name of freedom, thinking freedom is the production of black life, whose generativity has nothing to retrieve in the past, as if there were any pure thought that would redeem the murky present; the alteration is, by way of refiguring, creating a different reality altogether.

This is the suite that lacks a prescriptive form, and it is rupture because freedom is, in itself, a rupturous affair. It is creating other possibilities, in the intensification of the discursive shifts, what obliterates the strictures and edicts that come in the name of disciplinary orders and universal language, whose freedom is far out of the reality of black life, and entrenches its misery. The contrarian take of black thought, the critical disposition of Douglass, Morrison, Spillers, and Mingus, is the act, the effort of enacting fundamental change, the instituting of different ways of thinking, knowing, and doing. Giving premium to black life, engendering the modes through which it must be lived freely in the belly of unfreedom, makes the contrapuntal take its forever critical disposition to be what attests to the lived reality of living in unfreedom. It is in the denial of black life that the demands for this life, which is advocated to be in its free form, mean that black thought imprints itself.

Black thought is the living memory of what *was, is*, and *will be*. The past, present, and the future are sedimented. It is in this solid grounding, this thickening and compression of time that black thought is able to think through the long history of dehumanization, not as being episodic but as a continuum. The base of black life is that which Douglass, Morrison, Spillers, and Mingus are thinking and, in their thinking, memory work unfolds. It is in this unfolding that different mappings of reality come into being and refiguring means, as well, reading from and off the base. Of course, all this depends on what are the critical questions, concerns, provocations, and matters of black life that are urgent in order to be taken up.

The current conjuncture will always be the time of the now. It is not the time that has passed or that is yet to come. Black thought, in this figuring of what is forever urgent, is the discursive domain of the now. The call to act, then, by whatever means necessary, which is to say refiguring, is rightfully in this current conjuncture.

References

Agamben, Giorgio. 1998. *Homo Sacer: Sovereignty Power and Bare Life*, trans. D. Heller-Rozzen. Stanford: Stanford University Press.

_____. 2017. *Creation and Anarchy: The Work of Art and the Religion of Capitalism*. Stanford: Stanford University Press.

Alcoff, Linda M. 2010. "Sotomayor's Reasoning." *The Southern Journal of Philosophy* 8 (1): 122–138.

Althusser, Louis. 1971. "Ideology and Ideological State Apparatus (Notes Towards an Investigation)." In *On Ideology*, 1–60. London and New York: Verso.

Anderson, Melanie R. 2013. *Spectrality in the Novels of Toni Morrison*. Knoxville: University of Tennessee Press.

Baker, Houston A, Jr. 1984. *Blues, Ideology, and Afro-American Literature: A Vernacular Theory*. Chicago: University of Chicago Press

Baraka, Amiri (Leroi Jones). 1963. *Blues People: Negro Music in White America*. Westport: Greenwood Press.

Biehl, João. 2001. "Vita: Life in a Zone of Social Abandonment." *Social Text* 19 (3): 131–149.

Bogues, Anthony. 2010. *Empire of Liberty: Power, Desire, and Freedom*. Hanover: University Press of New England.

Butler, Judith. 2004. *Precarious Life: The Powers of Mourning and Violence*. London and New York: Verso.

Campt, Tina M. 2017. *Listening to Images*. Durham, NC: Duke University Press.

Carter, J. Kameron. 2008. *Race: A Theological Account*. Oxford: Oxford University Press.

Cervenak, Sarah J. 2006. "Against Traffic: De/formations of Race and Freedom in the Art of Adrian Piper." *Discourse* 28 (2–3): 114–129.

_____. 2015. *Wandering: Philosophical Performances of Racial and Sexual Freedom*. Durham, NC: Duke University Press.

_____. 2016. "Black Gathering: 'The Weight of Being' in Leonardo Drew's Sculpture." *Women and Performance* 26 (1): 1–16.

Chandler, Nahum D. 1996. "The Economy of Desedimentation: W. E. B. DuBois and the Discourses of the Negro." *Callaloo* 19 (1): 78–93.

_____. 2014. *X: The Problem of the Negro as the Problem for Thought*. New York: Fordham University Press.

Comaroff, Jean and John Comaroff. 1991. *Of Revelation and Revolution: Christianity, Colonialism, and Consciousness: Volume One*. Chicago: University of Chicago Press.

_____. 1997. *Of Revelation and Revolution: The Dialectics of Modernity on a South African Frontier: Volume Two*. Chicago: University of Chicago Press.

Crawley, Ashon T. 2016. *Blackpentacostal Breath: The Aesthetics of Possible*. New York: Fordham University Press.

Douglass, Frederick. 1969 [1855]. *My Bondage and My Freedom*. New York: Dover Publications.

_____. 1995 [1845]. *Narrative of the Life of Frederick Douglass*. New York: Dover Publications.

Du Bois, William E. B. 2015 [1903]. *The Soul of Black Folk*. New Haven: Yale University Press.

Edwards, Brent. H. 2017. *Epistrophies: Jazz and the Literary Imagination*. Cambridge, MA: Harvard University Press.

Fanon, Frantz. 1967. *Black Skin, White Masks*, trans. Charles L. Markman. New York: Grove Press.

Farley, Anthony P. 2005. "Perfecting Slavery." *Loyola University Chicago Law Journal* 36: 225–256.

Foucault, Michel. 1997. *Discipline and Punish: The Birth of the Prison*, trans. Alan Sheridan. London: Penguin Books.

Garréta, Anne F. 2005. "Autonomy and its Discontent," *South Atlantic Quarterly* 104 (4): 723–733.

Gilmore, Ruth W. 2002. "Fatal Couplings of Power and Difference: Notes on Racism and Geography." *The Professional Geographer* 54 (1): 15–24.

Glissant, Édouard. 1997. *Poetics of Relation*. Ann Arbor: University of Michigan Press.

Gordon, Lewis R. 1995. *Bad Faith and Antiblack Racism*. New York: Humanity Books.

_____. 2000. *Existentia Africana: Understanding Africana Existential Thought*. London: Routledge.

Gumbs, Alexis, P. 2016. *Spill: Scenes of Black Feminist Fugitivity*. Durham, NC: Duke University Press.

Hardt, Michael and Antonio Negri. 2009. *Commonwealth*. Cambridge, MA: The Belknap Press of Harvard University Press.

Hartman, Saidiya. 1997. *Scenes of Subjection: Terror, Slavery, Self-making in the Nineteenth-Century America*. Oxford: Oxford University Press.

_____. 2002. "The Time of Slavery." *The South Atlantic Quarterly* 101 (4): 757–777.

_____. 2016. "The Belly of the World: A Note on Black Women's Labor." *Souls* 18 (1): 166–167.

_____. 2019a. *Wayward Lives, Beautiful Experiments: Intimate Histories of Social Upheaval*. London: W. W. Norton and Co.

_____. 2019b. "Liner Notes for the Riot." *E-Flux Journal* 105, December: 1–3.

JanMohamed, Abdul R. 2005. *The Death-Bound-Subject: Richard Wright's Archaeology of Death*. Durham, NC: Duke University Press.

Judy, Ronald A. T. 1993. *(Dis)Forming the American Canon: African-Arabic Slave Narratives and the Vernacular*. Minneapolis: University of Minnesota Press.

_____. 2020. *Sentient Flesh: Thinking in Disorder, Poiēsis in Black*. Durham, NC: Duke University Press.

Mackey, Nathaniel. 1995. "Other: From Noun to Verb." From: *Jazz Among the Discourses*, ed. Krin Gabbard, 76–99. Durham, NC: Duke University Press.

McKittrick, Katherine. 2006. *Demonic Grounds: Black Women and the Cartographies of Struggle*. Minneapolis: University of Minnesota Press.

_____. 2018. *Paracritical Hinge: Essays, Talks, Notes, Interviews*. Iowa City: University of Iowa Press.

Maldonado-Torres, Nelson. 2007. "On Coloniality of Being: Contributions to the Development of a Concept." *Cultural Studies* 21 (2 and 3): 240–270.

_____. 2008. *Against War: Views from the Underside of Modernity*. Durham, NC: Duke University Press.

Marriott, David. 2015. "The Racialized Body." In *The Cambridge Companion to the Body in Literature*, eds David Hillman and Ulrika Maude, 163–176. Cambridge: Cambridge University Press.

Mbembe, Achille. 2001. *On the Postcolony*. Berkeley, CA: University of California Press.

Mingus, Charles. 1971. *Beneath the Underdog: His World as Composed by Mingus*. New York: Vintage Books.

Mignolo, Walter D. 2008. "Racism as We Sense it Today." *PMLA* 123 (5): 1737–1742.

———. 2011. *The Darker Side of Western Modernity: Global Futures, Decolonial Options*. Durham, NC: Duke University Press.

Morrison, Toni. 1992. *Playing in the Dark: Whiteness and the Literary Imagination*. New York: Vintage Books.

———. 1997. "Home." In *The House that Race Built: Black Americans, U.S. Terrain*, ed. Wahneema Lubiano, 3–12. New York: Pantheon Books.

———. 2019. *The Source of Self-Regard: Selected Essays, Speeches, and Meditations*. New York: Alfred A. Knopf.

Moten, Fred. 2003. *In the Break: The Aesthetics of the Black Radical Tradition*. Minneapolis: University of Minnesota Press.

———. 2013. "The Subprime and the Beautiful." *African Identities* 11 (2): 237–245.

———. 2017. *Black and Blur*. Durham, NC: Duke University Press.

———. 2018a. *Stolen Life*. Durham, NC: Duke University Press.

———. 2018b. *The Universal Machine*. Durham, NC: Duke University Press.

Moya, Paula M. L. 2011. "Who We Are and from Where We Speak." *Transmodernity* 1 (2): 79–94.

Mudimbe, V. Y. 1988. *The Invention of Africa: Gnosis, Philosophy, and the Order of Knowledge*. Bloomington and Indianapolis: Indiana University Press.

———. 1993. *The Idea of Africa*. Bloomington and Indianapolis: Indiana University Press.

———. 2003. *On African Fault Line: Meditation of the Politics of Alterity*. Scottsville: UKZN Press.

Nancy, Jean-Luc. 1996. "The Deleuzean Fold of Thought." In *Deleuze: A Critical Reader*, ed. Paul Patton and trans. Tom Gibson and Anthony Uhlmann, 107–113. Oxford: Blackwell Publishers.

Ndlovu-Gatsheni, Sabelo J. 2009. *The Ndebele Nation: Reflections on Hegemony, Memory and Historiography.* Pretoria: Unisa Press.

_____. 2012. "Beyond the Equator There are No Sins: Coloniality and Violence in Africa." *Journal of Developing Societies* 28 (4): 419–440.

_____. 2013a. *Coloniality of Power in Postcolonial Africa: Myths of Decolonization.* Dakar: CODESRIA.

_____. 2013b. *Empire, Global Coloniality and African Subjectivity.* New York and Oxford: Berghahn.

Noys, Benjamin. 2002. "Time of Death." *Angelaki* 7 (2): 51–59.

Okiji, Fumi. 2018. *Jazz as Critique: Adorno and Black Expression Revisited.* Stanford: Stanford University Press.

Patterson, Orlando. 1982. *Slavery and Social Death: A Comparative Study.* Cambridge, MA: Harvard University Press.

Pierpont, Claudia R. 2010. "Black, Brown, and Beige: Duke Ellington's Music and Race in America." *The New Yorker*, May 10.

Rios, Josh. 2017. "A Possible Future Returns to the Past." *Somatechnics* 7 (1): 59–73.

Robinson, Cedric J. 2000. *Black Marxism: The Making of the Black Radical Tradition.* Chapel Hill: University of North Carolina Press.

Rustin-Pascal, Nichole. 2017. *The Kind of Man I Am: Jazzmasculinity and the World of Charles Mingus Jr.* Middletown: Wesleyan University Press.

Santoro, Gene. 2000. *Myself When I am Real: The Life and Music of Charles Mingus.* Oxford and New York: Oxford University Press.

Santos, Boaventura de Sousa. 2007. "Beyond Abyssal Thinking: From Global Lines to Ecologies of Knowledges." *Review* 30 (1): 45–89.

Schmudde, Carol E. 1992. "The Haunting of 124." *African American Review* 26 (3): 409–416.

Sexton, Jarred. 2015. "Unbearable Blackness." *Cultural Critique* 90, Spring: 159–178.

Sharpe, Christina. 2010. *Monstrous Intimacies: Making Post-Slavery Subjects.* Durham, NC: Duke University Press.

_____. 2016. *In the Wake: On Blackness and Being.* Durham, NC: Duke University Press.

Spillers, Hortense J. 1987. "Mama's Baby, Papa's Maybe: An American Grammar Book." *Diacritics* 17 (2): 64–81.

_____. 1994. "The Crisis of the Negro Intellectual: A Post-Date." *boundary 2*, 21 (2): 65–116.

_____. 2003. *Black, White and Color: Essays on American Literature and Culture*. Chicago: University of Chicago Press.

_____. 2017. "Stuart Hall in this Moment." *Callaloo* 40 (1): 96–97.

Tadiar, Neferti X. M. 2015. "Decolonization, 'Race,' and Remaindered Life Under Empire," *Qui Parle* 23 (2): 135–160.

Terrefe, Selamawit D. 2018. "Speaking the Hieroglyph." *Theory and Event* 21 (1): 124–147.

Tlostanova, Madina. 2017. "Transcending the Human/Non-Human Divide: The Geo-politics and Body-politics of Being and Perception, and Decolonial Art." *Angelaki* 22 (2): 25–37.

wa Thiong'o, Ngũgĩ. 1987. *Decolonizing the Mind: The Politics of Language in African Literature*. London: James Currey.

Walcott, Derek. 1998. *What the Twilight Says*. New York: Farrar, Straus and Giroux.

Walker, Corey D. 2011. "'How Does it Feel to be a Problem?' (Local) Knowledge, Human Interests, and the Ethics of Opacity," *Transmodernity* 1 (2): 104–119.

Weheliye, Alexander G. 2005. *Phonographies: Grooves in Sonic Afro-Modernity*. Durham, NC: Duke University Press.

_____. 2014. *Habeas Viscus: Racializing Assemblages, Biopolitics, and Black Feminist Theories of the Human*. Durham, NC: Duke University Press.

Wilderson, Frank B. III. 2003. "Gramsci's Black Marx: Whither the Slave in Civil Society?" *Social Identities* 9 (2): 225–240.

_____. 2010. *Red, White, and Black: Cinema and the Structure of US Antagonisms*. Durham, NC: Duke University Press.

Wright, Michelle. 2004. *Becoming Black: Creating Identity in the Age of Diaspora*. Durham, NC: Duke University Press.

Index